SOLICITORS' ACCOUNTS MANUAL

Ninth Edition

SOLICITORS' ACCOUNTS MANUAL

NINTH EDITION

The Law Society

© The Law Society 2004

ISBN 1 85328 907 8

1st edition 1986
2nd edition 1987
3rd edition 1990
4th edition 1992
5th edition 1994
6th edition 1996
7th edition 1999
8th edition 2001
9th edition 2004
Reprinted 2004, 2005

The material in Annex A is Crown copyright.

This 9th edition published by
The Law Society
113 Chancery Lane
London WC2A 1PL

Typeset by Columns Design Ltd, Reading, Berkshire

Printed and bound in Great Britain by
TJ International Ltd, Padstow, Cornwall

Contents

Preface

This is the ninth edition of the *Solicitors' Accounts Manual*. It reproduces Chapter 28 from the Guide Online (www.guide-on-line.lawsociety.org.uk), which is an updated version of Chapter 28 in *The Guide to the Professional Conduct of Solicitors* (eighth edition, published in 1999 by the Law Society).

Annex B, which contains the Solicitors' Accounts Rules 1998, includes all changes made to the rules since publication of the *Guide* up to 17th March 2004:

- from 6th January 2000, the Law Society has enhanced monitoring powers, and solicitors may use a building society share account (as well as a deposit account) for a client account;
- from 22nd May 2000, provision has been made for registered European lawyers who are now also subject to the rules;
- excluding any period before 1st September 2000, the reporting accountant is required to note on the report whether or not there appears to have been indemnity insurance for the period covered by the report;
- from 6th April 2001, provision has been made for members of recognised bodies which are limited liability partnerships, who are now also subject to the rules;
- from 1st December 2001, the reporting accountant is no longer required to confirm compliance with any rule relating to investment business;
- from 13th January 2003, an accounting period may be changed to a period longer than twelve months only if the Law Society receives written notice by a specified time – see rule 36(4);
- from 17th March 2004, the following changes apply:
    - note (ix) to rule 15 has been updated to reflect the view of the Solicitors' Disciplinary Tribunal that the provision of banking facilities through a client account does not form part of a solicitor's practice;
    - new rule 21(2), and new notes (vii)–(x), deal with regular payments from the Legal Services Commission under its civil and criminal contracting schemes (the new rule must be implemented by 1st May 2005 but firms may continue to operate under the interim guidance until 30th April 2005);
    - an amended rule 32(10), and new notes (xiv)–(xvii), permit the retention of digital images of paid client account cheques in place of the original paper cheques.

Relevant extracts from the Solicitors' Overseas Practice Rules 1990, also updated, appear as an additional Annex F in this book (Annex 9A in the *Guide*, an updated version of which appears in the Guide Online).

From 17th March 2004, a solicitor will be exempt from the accounts provisions of the overseas practice rules, and the obligation to deliver an accountant's report, if:

- a controlling majority of the partners in the firm are lawyers of other jurisdictions;
- UK lawyers do not form the largest national group of lawyers in the partnership; and
- the solicitor has held or received client money or controlled trust money only by virtue of being a partner in the overseas firm (a solicitor who holds or receives client money or controlled trust money as a named trustee continues to be subject to the accounts provisions).

The exemption applies only to overseas practice, not to practice in England and Wales.

The Law Society
May 2004

PART VI – FINANCIAL REGULATIONS

Chapter 28

Accounts

28.01   Operation of the accounts rules

[Deleted – since 1st May 2000, solicitors have had to operate under the Solicitors' Accounts Rules 1998.]

28.02   The 1998 rules

The Solicitors' Accounts Rules 1998 (see Annex B) came into effect on 22nd July 1998. The 1998 rules consolidate all rules and guidance relating to solicitors' accounts, including the requirements for an accountant's report. The consolidation of rules and guidance means that this chapter is relatively short, as the 1998 rules contain all the guidance previously set out in Chapter 28 in the seventh edition of the Guide. The 1998 rules start with a list of contents and conclude with an index.

28.03 Continued use of the 1991 rules

[Deleted – since 1st May 2000, solicitors have had to operate under the Solicitors' Accounts Rules 1998.]

28.04 New provisions in the 1998 rules

[Deleted – since 1st May 2000, solicitors have had to operate under the Solicitors' Accounts Rules 1998.]

28.05 Accounts of an overseas practice

1. Solicitors who practise outside England and Wales are bound by the Solicitors' Overseas Practice Rules 1990 in respect of their accounts, accountant's reports and investigation of accounts. The relevant rules are rules 12 (accounts), 13 (trust accounts) and 16 (accountants' reports) – see Annex 9A [of the *Guide*, or refer to Annex F of this book]. The requirements of these rules embody the general principles of the Accounts Rules, but are less detailed and less onerous. The Law Society sends out a form of accountant's report for overseas practices directly to solicitors, but it is not compulsory to use this form of report.

2. The Solicitors' Overseas Practice Rules – and thus the relevant accounts provisions – do not apply to a registered European lawyer's practice outside the UK. They do, however, apply to a registered European lawyer's practice from an office in Scotland or Northern Ireland, and references to a solicitor in paragraph 3 below must be read as including a registered European lawyer practising from an office in Scotland or Northern Ireland.

3. The accounts provisions apply to

   • a solicitor who holds or receives client money or controlled trust money as a sole principal;

   • a solicitor who holds or receives client money or controlled trust money as a named trustee;

   • a solicitor who holds or receives client money or controlled trust money as a partner in a partnership which is not an LLP with separate legal personality, if solicitors are a controlling majority or 50% of the partners, or if UK lawyers form the largest national group of lawyers in the partnership;

- a solicitor who is a partner in a partnership which is an overseas LLP with separate legal personality, if the partnership holds or receives client money or controlled trust money and a controlling majority of the partners are solicitors;

- a solicitor who is a director and/or owner of a corporate practice, if the corporate practice holds or receives client money or controlled trust money and a controlling majority of the owners of the practice are solicitors;

- a recognised body which is incorporated in England and Wales, if it holds or receives client money or controlled trust money; and

- a recognised body which is incorporated outside England and Wales, if it holds or receives client money or controlled trust money and if a controlling majority of its owners are solicitors.

4. For guidance on how the overseas accounts provisions affect a solicitor who is a partner in a limited liability partnership formed under US law, see Annex 9C [of the Guide Online at www.guide-on-line.lawsociety.org.uk, reproduced here as Annex G].

28.06 Controlled trust accounts of an overseas practice

1. The Solicitors' Overseas Practice Rules 1990 include a requirement for reporting accountants to make a test check of controlled trust accounts. This applies to trusts where

- a solicitor in sole practice is a sole trustee or co-trustee only with one or more employees;

- a solicitor partner who is subject to rules 13 and 16 is sole trustee or co-trustee only with one or more partners or employees;

- a recognised body which is subject to rules 13 and 16 is sole trustee or co-trustee only with one or more of its officers or employees (or one or more of its members or employees if it is an LLP); and

- a solicitor director or owner of a corporate practice who is subject to rules 13 and 16 by virtue of rule 9(3)(a) to (c), where the corporate practice is sole trustee or co-trustee only with one or more of its directors and/or owners and/or employees, or the solicitor is sole trustee or co-trustee only with one or more of the other directors and/or owners and/or employees;

- a solicitor partner in an overseas LLP with separate legal personality is subject to rules 13 and 16 by virtue of rule 9(3)(d), where the LLP is sole trustee or co-trustee only with one or more of the partners and/or employees, or the solicitor is sole trustee or co-trustee only with one or more of the other partners and/or employees; and

- an assistant solicitor who is a controlled trustee by virtue of any of the above provisions, or who is a sole trustee.

2. The Solicitors' Overseas Practice Rules – and thus the relevant accounts provisions and the test checks – do not apply to a registered European lawyer's practice outside the UK. They do, however, apply to a registered European lawyer's practice from an office in Scotland or Northern Ireland, and references to a solicitor in paragraph 1 above must be read as including a registered European lawyer practising from an office in Scotland or Northern Ireland.

3. The following notes apply where there are one or more controlled trusts.

    (a) The accountant is required to make a test check of only a limited number of accounts and files relating to controlled trusts. The number and selection of controlled trust accounts included in the examination is left to the discretion of the reporting accountant. The fact that an accountant (not necessarily the reporting accountant) is already engaged in the management of a particular trust may well be relevant to the reporting accountant's decision whether or not to do test checks in respect of that particular trust, especially if annual accounts are prepared by the trust's accountant.

    (b) There is no question of the reporting accountant having to check that the investments made in respect of the trust are appropriate. Accountants may find it useful to refer to the series of checks contained in rule 42 of the Solicitors' Accounts Rules 1998 (see Annex B). The overseas practice rules require solicitors practising overseas either to keep a central register of controlled trusts or to keep the accounts relating to controlled trusts together centrally.

    (c) The solicitor's duty to keep separate accounting records for each controlled trust will in many cases be discharged by simply retaining bank statements, etc., provided that the narrative is sufficient to understand the various movements on the account. However, in the case of a trust which is particularly complex or is likely to be protracted, formal records should be kept.

    (d) The reporting accountant should select what he or she considers to be a suitable sample of controlled trust accounts and it may then be appropriate to make a correspondingly reduced number of checks in respect of the client and other accounts. However, where trust work forms all or the major part of the business of a practice, the scale of work carried out by the reporting accountant will be on a par with that undertaken for a firm carrying out a similar amount of client account business.

    (e) Where a trust company which is operated as an overseas corporate practice holds shares in investment companies established for individual clients, the reporting accountant is simply required to check the book-keeping system and accounting entries relating to the operations of the trust company itself, including its purchase of shares in individual investment companies. The operation of the investment companies themselves falls outside the scope of the accountant's report.

4. Money held by a hived-off overseas trust company, i.e. a company not forming part of a solicitors' practice and not regulated by the Society as a solicitors' practice, falls outside the scope of the accountant's report. However, an overseas trust company which is run as a corporate practice in accordance with rule 9(1)(a) or (b) of the overseas practice rules is subject to the accounts provisions and the test checks if it has a controlling majority of solicitor owners.

28.07 Waivers for overseas practices

If local conditions make it difficult for a solicitor to comply with the Solicitors' Overseas Practice Rules 1990, application may be made to Professional Ethics for a waiver under rule 19 [see Annex F of this book].

Annex A

Solicitors Act 1974

sections 34 and 85 (accountants' reports and bank accounts)

(with consolidated amendments to October 2003)

---

34. Accountants' reports

(1)   Every solicitor shall once in each period of twelve months ending with 31st October, unless the Council are satisfied that it is unnecessary for him to do so, deliver to the Society, whether by post or otherwise, a report signed by an accountant (in this section referred to as an 'accountant's report') and containing such information as may be prescribed by rules made by the Council under this section.

(2)   An accountant's report shall be delivered to the Society not more than six months (or such other period as may be prescribed by rules made under this section) after the end of the accounting period for the purposes of that report.

(3)   Subject to any rules made under this section, the accounting period for the purposes of an accountant's report –

    (a)   shall begin at the expiry of the last preceding accounting period for which an accountant's report has been delivered;

    (b)   shall cover not less than twelve months; and

    (c)   where possible, consistently with the preceding provisions of this section, shall correspond to a period or consecutive periods for which the accounts of the solicitor or his firm are ordinarily made up.

(4)   The Council shall make rules to give effect to the provisions of this section, and those rules shall prescribe –

    (a)   the qualification to be held by an accountant by whom an accountant's report is given;

    (b)   the information to be contained in an accountant's report;

    (c)   the nature and extent of the examination to be made by an accountant of the books and accounts of a solicitor or his firm and of any other relevant documents with a view to the signing of an accountant's report;

    (d)   the form of an accountant's report; and

    (e)   the evidence, if any, which shall satisfy the Council that the delivery of an accountant's report is unnecessary and the cases in which such evidence is or is not required.

(5)   Rules under this section may include provision –

(a)   permitting in such special circumstances as may be defined by the rules a different accounting period from that specified in subsection (3); and

(b)   regulating any matters of procedure or matters incidental, ancillary or supplemental to the provisions of this section.

(5A) Without prejudice to the generality of subsection (5)(b), rules under this section may make provision requiring a solicitor in advance of delivering an accountant's report to notify the Society of the period which is to be the accounting period for the purposes of that report in accordance with the preceding provisions of this section.

(6)   If any solicitor fails to comply with the provisions of this section or of any rules made under it, a complaint in respect of that failure may be made to the Tribunal by or on behalf of the Society.

(7)   A certificate under the hand of the Secretary of the Society shall, until the contrary is proved, be evidence that a solicitor has or, as the case may be, has not delivered to the Society an accountant's report or supplied any evidence required under this section or any rules made under it.

(8)   Where a solicitor is exempt from rules under section 32 –

(a)   nothing in this section shall apply to him unless he takes out a practising certificate;

(b)   an accountant's report shall in no case deal with books, accounts or documents kept by him in the course of employment by virtue of which he is exempt from those rules; and

(c)   no examination shall be made of any such books, accounts and documents under any rules made under this section.

[NOTES

1.   For a similar provision in relation to registered foreign lawyers see paragraph 8 of Schedule 14 to the Courts and Legal Services Act 1990.

2.   By virtue of section 89(3) of the Courts and Legal Services Act 1990 the power to make rules under section 34 is also exercisable in relation to registered foreign lawyers.

3.   For the application of section 34 to a recognised body (i.e. an incorporated practice recognised under section 9 of the Administration of Justice Act 1985) see paragraph 5 of Schedule 2 to the Administration of Justice Act 1985.

4.   By virtue of section 9(2)(f) of the Administration of Justice Act 1985 rules made under section 34 may be made to have effect in relation to a recognised body.]

85.   Bank accounts

Where a solicitor keeps an account with a bank or a building society in pursuance of rules under section 32 –

(a)   the bank or society shall not incur any liability, or be under any obligation to make any inquiry, or be deemed to have any knowledge of any right of any person to any money paid or credited to the account, which it would not incur or be under or be deemed to have in the case of an account kept by a person entitled absolutely to all the money paid or credited to it; and

(b)   the bank or society shall not have any recourse or right against money standing to the credit of the account, in respect of any liability of the solicitor to the bank or society, other than a liability in connection with the account.

[NOTES

1.   For the application of section 85 to a recognised body see paragraph 31 of Schedule 2 to the Administration of Justice Act 1985.

2.   Section 85 is extended to client accounts of multi-national partnerships by the Registered Foreign Lawyers Order 1991 (S.I. 1991 no. 2831).]

Annex B

Solicitors' Accounts Rules 1998

(with consolidated amendments to 17th March 2004)

[For Index to the accounts rules, see p. 78]

Made by: the Council of the Law Society with the concurrence, where requisite, of the Master of the Rolls;

date: 22nd July 1998;

authority: sections 32, 33A, 34 and 37 of the Solicitors Act 1974 and section 9 of the Administration of Justice Act 1985;

replacing: the Solicitors' Accounts Rules 1991, the Solicitors' Accounts (Legal Aid Temporary Provision) Rule 1992 and the Accountant's Report Rules 1991;

regulating: the accounts of solicitors, registered European lawyers, registered foreign lawyers and recognised bodies in respect of their English and Welsh practices.

CONTENTS: Page

PART A – GENERAL

Rule 1 – Principles

The following principles must be observed. A *solicitor* must:

(a) comply with the requirements of practice rule 1 as to the *solicitor's* integrity, the duty to act in the *client's* best interests, and the good repute of the *solicitor* and the *solicitor's* profession;

(b) keep other people's money separate from money belonging to the *solicitor* or the practice;

(c) keep other people's money safely in a *bank* or *building society* account identifiable as a *client account* (except when the rules specifically provide otherwise);

(d) use each *client's* money for that *client's* matters only;

(e) use *controlled trust money* for the purposes of that *trust* only;

(f) establish and maintain proper accounting systems, and proper internal controls over those systems, to ensure compliance with the rules;

(g) keep proper accounting records to show accurately the position with regard to the money held for each *client* and each *controlled trust*;

(h) account for interest on other people's money in accordance with the rules;

(i) co-operate with the *Society* in checking compliance with the rules; and

(j) deliver annual accountant's reports as required by the rules.

Rule 2 – Interpretation

(1) The rules are to be interpreted in the light of the notes.

(2) In the rules, unless the context otherwise requires:

    (a) "accounting period" has the meaning given in rule 36;

    (b) "agreed fee" has the meaning given in rule 19(5);

    (c) "bank" means an institution authorised under the Banking Act 1987 (which includes a European authorised institution), the Post Office in the exercise of its powers to provide banking services, or the Bank of England;

    (d) "building society" means a building society within the meaning of the Building Societies Act 1986;

    (e) "client" means the person for whom a *solicitor* acts;

    (f) "client account" has the meaning given in rule 14(2);

    (g) "client money" has the meaning given in rule 13;

    (h) a "controlled trust" arises when:

        (i) a *solicitor of the Supreme Court* or *registered European lawyer* is the sole *trustee* of a *trust*, or co-*trustee* only with one or more of his or her *partners* or employees;

(ii)   a *registered foreign lawyer* who practises in *partnership* with a *solicitor of the Supreme Court* or *registered European lawyer* is, by virtue of being a *partner* in that *partnership*, the sole *trustee* of a *trust*, or co-*trustee* only with one or more of the other *partners* or employees of that *partnership*;

(iii) a *recognised body* which is a company is the sole *trustee* of a *trust*, or co-*trustee* only with one or more of the *recognised body's* officers or employees; or

(iv) a *recognised body* which is a limited liability partnership is the sole *trustee* of a *trust*, or co-*trustee* only with one or more of the *recognised body's* members or employees;

and "controlled trustee" means a *trustee* of a *controlled trust* (see also paragraph (y) below on the meaning of "trustee" and "trust");

(i)   "controlled trust money" has the meaning given in rule 13;

(j)   "costs" means a *solicitor's* fees and *disbursements*;

(k)   "disbursement" means any sum spent or to be spent by a *solicitor* on behalf of the *client* or *controlled trust* (including any VAT element);

(l)   "fees" of a *solicitor* means the *solicitor's* own charges or profit costs (including any VAT element);

(m) "general client account" has the meaning given in rule 14(5)(b);

(n)   "mixed payment" has the meaning given in rule 20(1);

(o)   "non-solicitor employer" means an employer who or which is not a *solicitor*;

(p)   "office account" means an account of the *solicitor* or the practice for holding *office money*, or other means of holding *office money* (for example, the office cash box);

(q)   "office money" has the meaning given in rule 13;

(qa) "partnership" means an unincorporated partnership and does not include a limited liability partnership, and "partner" is to be construed accordingly;

(r)   "principal" means:

(i)   a sole practitioner;

(ii)   a *partner* or a person held out as a *partner* (including a "salaried" or "associate" *partner*);

(iii) the principal *solicitor* (or any one of the principal *solicitors*) in an in-house practice (for example, in a law centre or in commerce and industry);

(s)   "professional disbursement" means the fees of counsel or other lawyer, or of a professional or other agent or expert instructed by the *solicitor*;

(t)   "recognised body" means a company or limited liability partnership recognised by the *Society* under section 9 of the Administration of Justice Act 1985;

(ta)   "registered European lawyer" means a person registered by the *Society* under regulation 17 of the European Communities (Lawyer's Practice) Regulations 2000;

(u)   "registered foreign lawyer" means a person registered by the *Society* under section 89 of the Courts and Legal Services Act 1990;

(ua)   "regular payment" has the meaning given in rule 21;

(v)   "separate designated client account" has the meaning given in rule 14(5)(a);

(w)   "Society" means the Law Society of England and Wales;

(x)   "solicitor" means a *solicitor of the Supreme Court*; and for the purposes of these rules also includes: a *registered European lawyer*; a *registered foreign lawyer* practising in *partnership* with a *solicitor of the Supreme Court* or *registered European lawyer* or as the director of a *recognised body* which is a company or as a member of a *recognised body* which is a limited liability partnership; a *recognised body*; and a *partnership* including at least one *solicitor of the Supreme Court*, *registered European lawyer* or *recognised body*;

(xa)   "solicitor of the Supreme Court" means an individual who is a solicitor of the Supreme Court of England and Wales;

(y)   "trustee" includes a personal representative (i.e. an executor or an administrator), and "trust" includes the duties of a personal representative; and

(z)   "without delay" means, in normal circumstances, either on the day of receipt or on the next working day.

Notes

(i)   Although many of the rules are expressed as applying to an individual solicitor, the effect of the definition of "solicitor" in rule 2(2)(x) is that the rules apply equally to all those who carry on a practice and to the practice itself. See also rule 4(1)(a) (persons governed by the rules) and rule 5 (persons exempt from the rules).

(ii)   A client account must be at a bank or building society's branch in England and Wales – see rule 14(4).

(iii)   For the full definition of a "European authorised institution" (rule 2(2)(c)), see the Banking Coordination (Second Council Directive) Regulations 1992 (S.I. 1992 no. 3218).

(iv)   The definition of a controlled trust (rule 2(2)(h)), which derives from statute, gives rise to some anomalies. For example, a partner, assistant solicitor or consultant acting as sole trustee will be a controlled trustee. So will a sole solicitor trustee who is a director of a recognised body which is a company, or a member of a recognised body which is a limited liability partnership. Two or more partners acting as trustees will be controlled trustees. However, two or more assistant solicitors or consultants acting as trustees will fall outside the definition, as will two or more directors of a recognised body which is a company, or two or more members of a recognised body which is a limited liability partnership. In these cases, if the matter is dealt with through the practice, the partners (or the recognised body) will hold any money as client money.

(iva)   Exceptionally, where a trust is handled by registered European lawyers, the trustees might be two partners at the firm's head office in the home state who are not directly subject to the rules. Money in the trust should be held by the firm as client money. However, it should be treated as if it were controlled trust money in relation to choice of account, accounting for interest, etc., to ensure that there is no breach of duty by the trustees.

(v)   The fees of interpreters, translators, process servers, surveyors, estate agents, etc., instructed by the solicitor are professional disbursements (see rule 2(2)(s)). Travel agents' charges are not professional disbursements.

(vi)   The general definition of "office account" is wide (see rule 2(2)(p)). However, rule 19(1)(b) (receipt and transfer of costs) and rule 21(1)(b) and 21(2)(b) (payments from the Legal Services Commission) specify that certain money is to be placed in an office account at a bank or building society.

(vii)   An index is attached to the rules but it does not form part of the rules. For the status of the flowchart (Appendix 1) and the chart dealing with special situations (Appendix 2), see note (xiii) to rule 13.

Rule 3 – Geographical scope

The rules apply to practice carried on from an office in England and Wales.

Note

Practice carried on from an office outside England and Wales is governed by the Solicitors' Overseas Practice Rules.

Rule 4 – Persons governed by the rules

(1)   The rules apply to:

    (a)   *solicitors of the Supreme Court* who are:

        (i)   sole practitioners;

        (ii)   *partners* in a practice, or held out as *partners* (including "salaried" and "associate" *partners*);

        (iii)   assistants, associates, consultants or locums in a private practice;

        (iv)   employed as in-house *solicitors* (for example, in a law centre or in commerce and industry);

        (v)   directors of *recognised bodies* which are companies; or

        (vi)   members of *recognised bodies* which are limited liability partnerships;

    (aa)   *registered European lawyers* who are:

        (i)   sole practitioners;

        (ii)   *partners* in a practice, or held out as *partners* (including "salaried" and "associate" *partners*);

        (iii)   assistants, associates, consultants or locums in a private practice;

        (iv)   employed as in-house lawyers (for example, in a law centre or in commerce and industry);

        (v)   directors of *recognised bodies* which are companies; or

        (vi)   members of *recognised bodies* which are limited liability partnerships;

(b)   *registered foreign lawyers* who are:

    (i)   practising in *partnership* with *solicitors of the Supreme Court* or *registered European lawyers*, or held out as *partners* (including "salaried" and "associate" *partners*) of *solicitors of the Supreme Court* or *registered European lawyers*;

    (ii)   directors of *recognised bodies* which are companies; or

    (iii)   members of *recognised bodies* which are limited liability partnerships; and

(c)   *recognised bodies*.

(2)   Part F of the rules (accountants' reports) also applies to reporting accountants.

Notes

(i)   In practical terms, the rules also bind anyone else working in a practice, such as cashiers and non-lawyer fee-earners. Non-compliance by any member of staff will lead to the principals being in breach of the rules – see rule 6. Misconduct by an employee can also lead to an order of the Solicitors' Disciplinary Tribunal under section 43 of the Solicitors Act 1974 imposing restrictions on his or her employment.

(ii)   Solicitors who have held or received client money or controlled trust money, but no longer do so, whether or not they continue in practice, continue to be bound by some of the rules – for instance:

    ▶   rule 7 (duty to remedy breaches);

    ▶   rule 19(2), and note (xi) to rule 19, rule 32(8) to (15) and rule 33 (retention of records);

    ▶   rule 34 (production of records);

    ▶   Part F (accountants' reports), and in particular rule 35(1) and rule 36(5) (delivery of final report), and rule 38(2) and rule 46 (retention of records).

(iii)   The rules do not cover a solicitor's trusteeships carried on in a purely personal capacity outside any legal practice. It will normally be clear from the terms of the appointment whether the solicitor is being appointed trustee in a purely personal capacity or in his or her professional capacity. If a solicitor is charging for the work, it is clearly being done as solicitor. Use of professional stationery may also indicate that the work is being done in a professional capacity.

(iv)   A solicitor who wishes to retire from private practice must make a decision about any professional trusteeship. There are three possibilities:

    (a)   continue to act as a professional trustee (as evidenced by, for instance, charging for work done, or by continuing to use the title "solicitor" in connection with the trust). In this case, the solicitor must continue to hold a practising certificate, and money subject to the trust must continue to be dealt with in accordance with the rules;

    (b)   continue to act as trustee, but in a purely personal capacity. In this case, the solicitor must stop charging for the work, and must not be held out as a solicitor (unless this is qualified by words such as "non-practising" or "retired") in connection with the trust;

    (c)   cease to be a trustee.

Rule 5 – Persons exempt from the rules

The rules do not apply to:

(a)   a *solicitor* when practising as an employee of:

    (i)   a local authority;

    (ii) statutory undertakers;

    (iii) a body whose accounts are audited by the Comptroller and Auditor General;

    (iv) the Duchy of Lancaster;

    (v) the Duchy of Cornwall; or

    (vi) the Church Commissioners; or

(b)   a *solicitor* who practises as the Solicitor of the City of London; or

(c)   a *solicitor* when carrying out the functions of:

    (i)   a coroner or other judicial office; or

    (ii) a sheriff or under-sheriff.

Notes

(i)   "Statutory undertakers" means:

    (a)   any persons authorised by any enactment to carry on any railway, light railway, tramway, road transport, water transport, canal, inland navigation, dock, harbour, pier or lighthouse undertaking or any undertaking for the supply of hydraulic power; and

    (b)   any licence holder within the meaning of the Electricity Act 1989, any public gas supplier, any water or sewerage undertaker, the Environment Agency, any public telecommunications operator, the Post Office, the Civil Aviation Authority and any relevant airport operator within the meaning of Part V of the Airports Act 1986.

(ii)   "Local authority" means any of those bodies which are listed in section 270 of the Local Government Act 1972 or in section 21(1) of the Local Government and Housing Act 1989.

Rule 6 – Principals' responsibility for compliance

All the *principals* in a practice must ensure compliance with the rules by the *principals* themselves and by everyone else working in the practice. This duty also extends to the directors of a *recognised body* which is a company, or to the members of a *recognised body* which is a limited liability partnership, and to the *recognised body* itself.

Rule 7 – Duty to remedy breaches

(1)   Any breach of the rules must be remedied promptly upon discovery. This includes the replacement of any money improperly withheld or withdrawn from a *client account*.

(2)   In a private practice, the duty to remedy breaches rests not only on the person causing the breach, but also on all the *principals* in the practice. This duty extends to replacing missing *client money* or *controlled trust money* from the *principals'* own resources, even if the money has been misappropriated by an employee or fellow *principal*, and whether or not a claim is subsequently made on the Solicitors' Indemnity or Compensation Funds or on the firm's insurance.

(3)   In the case of a *recognised body*, this duty falls on the *recognised body* itself.

Note

For payment of interest when money should have been held in a client account but was not, see rule 24(2).

Rule 8 – Controlled trustees

A *solicitor* who in the course of practice acts as a *controlled trustee* must treat the *controlled trust money* as if it were *client money*, except when the rules provide to the contrary.

Note

The following are examples of controlled trust money being treated differently from client money:

► rule 18 (controlled trust money withheld from a client account) – special provisions for controlled trusts, in place of rules 16 and 17 (which apply to client money);

► rule 19(2), and note (xi) to rule 19 – original bill etc., to be kept on file, in addition to central record or file of copy bills;

► rule 23, note (v) and rule 32, note (ii)(d) – controlled trustees may delegate to an outside manager the day to day keeping of accounts of the business or property portfolio of an estate or trust;

► rule 24(7), and note (x) to rule 24 – interest;

► rule 32(7) – quarterly reconciliations.

Rule 9 – Liquidators, trustees in bankruptcy, Court of Protection receivers and trustees of occupational pension schemes

(1) A *solicitor* who in the course of practice acts as

► a liquidator,

► a trustee in bankruptcy,

► a Court of Protection receiver, or

► a trustee of an occupational pension scheme which is subject to section 47(1)(a) of the Pensions Act 1995 (appointment of an auditor) **and** section 49(1) (separate bank account) **and** regulations under section 49(2)(b) (books and records),

must comply with:

(a) the appropriate statutory rules or regulations;

(b) the principles set out in rule 1; and

(c) the requirements of paragraphs (2) to (4) below;

and will then be deemed to have satisfactorily complied with the Solicitors' Accounts Rules.

(2) In respect of any records kept under the appropriate statutory rules, there must also be compliance with:

(a)   rule 32(8) – bills and notifications of costs;

(b)   rule 32(9)(c) – retention of records;

(c)   rule 32(12) – centrally kept records;

(d)   rule 34 – production of records; and

(e)   rule 42(1)(l) and (p) – reporting accountant to check compliance.

(3)   If a liquidator or trustee in bankruptcy uses any of the practice's *client accounts* for holding money pending transfer to the Insolvency Services Account or to a local bank account authorised by the Secretary of State, he or she must comply with the Solicitors' Accounts Rules in all respects whilst the money is held in the *client account*.

(4)   If the appropriate statutory rules or regulations do not govern the holding or receipt of *client money* in a particular situation (for example, money below a certain limit), the *solicitor* must comply with the Solicitors' Accounts Rules in all respects in relation to that money.

Notes

(i)   The Insolvency Regulations 1986 (S.I. 1986 no. 994) regulate liquidators and trustees in bankruptcy.

(ii)   The Court of Protection Rules 1994 (S.I. 1994 no. 3046) regulate Court of Protection receivers.

(iii)   Money held or received by solicitor liquidators, trustees in bankruptcy and Court of Protection receivers is client money but, because of the statutory rules and rule 9(1), it will not normally be kept in a client account. If for any reason it is held in a client account, the Solicitors' Accounts Rules apply to that money for the time it is so held (see rule 9(3) and (4)).

(iv)   Money held or received by solicitor trustees of occupational pension schemes is either client money or controlled trust money but, because of the statutory rules and rule 9(1), it will not normally be kept in a client account. If for any reason it is held in a client account, the Solicitors' Accounts Rules apply to that money for the time it is so held (see rule 9(4)).

Rule 10 – Joint accounts

(1)   If a *solicitor* acting in a *client's* matter holds or receives money jointly with the *client*, another *solicitor's* practice or another third party, the rules in general do not apply, but the following must be complied with:

(a)   rule 32(8) – bills and notifications of costs;

(b)   rule 32(9)(b)(ii) – retention of statements and passbooks;

(c)   rule 32(13) – centrally kept records;

(d)   rule 34 – production of records; and

(e)   rule 42(1)(m) and (p) – reporting accountant to check compliance.

Operation of the joint account by the solicitor only

(2)   If the joint account is operated only by the *solicitor*, the *solicitor* must ensure that he or she receives the statements from the *bank*, *building society* or other financial institution, and has possession of any passbooks.

Shared operation of the joint account

(3)   If the *solicitor* shares the operation of the joint account with the *client*, another *solicitor's* practice or another third party, the *solicitor* must:

   (a)   ensure that he or she receives the statements or duplicate statements from the *bank*, *building society* or other financial institution and retains them in accordance with rule 32(9)(b)(ii); and

   (b)   ensure that he or she either has possession of any passbooks, or takes copies of the passbook entries before handing any passbook to the other signatory, and retains them in accordance with rule 32(9)(b)(ii).

Operation of the joint account by the other account holder

(4)   If the joint account is operated solely by the other account holder, the *solicitor* must ensure that he or she receives the statements or duplicate statements from the *bank*, *building society* or other financial institution and retains them in accordance with rule 32(9)(b)(ii).

Note

Although a joint account is not a client account, money held in a joint account is client money.

Rule 11 – Operation of a client's own account

(1)   If a *solicitor* in the course of practice operates a *client's* own account as signatory (for example, as donee under a power of attorney), the rules in general do not apply, but the following must be complied with:

   (a)   rule 33(1) to (3) – accounting records for clients' own accounts;

   (b)   rule 34 – production of records; and

   (c)   rule 42(1)(n) and (p) – reporting accountant to check compliance.

Operation by the solicitor only

(2)   If the account is operated by the *solicitor* only, the *solicitor* must ensure that he or she receives the statements from the *bank*, *building society* or other financial institution, and has possession of any passbooks.

Shared operation of the account

(3)   If the *solicitor* shares the operation of the account with the *client* or a co-attorney outside the *solicitor's* practice, the *solicitor* must:

   (a)   ensure that he or she receives the statements or duplicate statements from the *bank*, *building society* or other financial institution and retains them in accordance with rule 33(1) to (3); and

   (b)   ensure that he or she either has possession of any passbooks, or takes copies of the passbook entries before handing any passbook to the *client* or co-attorney, and retains them in accordance with rule 33(1) to (3).

Operation of the account for a limited purpose

(4)   If the *solicitor* is given authority (whether as attorney or otherwise) to operate the account for a limited purpose only, such as the taking up of a share rights issue during the *client's* temporary absence, the *solicitor* need not receive statements or possess passbooks, provided that he or she retains details of all cheques drawn or paid in, and retains copies of all passbook entries, relating to the transaction, and retains them in accordance with rule 33(1) and (2).

Application

(5)   This rule applies only to *solicitors* in private practice.

Notes

(i)   Money held in a client's own account (under a power of attorney or otherwise) is not "client money" for the purpose of the rules because it is not "held or received" by the solicitor. If the solicitor closes the account and receives the closing balance, this becomes client money and must be paid into a client account, unless the client instructs to the contrary in accordance with rule 16(1)(a).

(ii)   A solicitor who merely pays money into a client's own account, or helps the client to complete forms in relation to such an account, is not "operating" the account.

(iii)   A solicitor executor who operates the deceased's account (whether before or after the grant of probate) will be subject to the limited requirements of rule 11. If the account is subsequently transferred into the solicitor's name, or a new account is opened in the solicitor's name, the solicitor will have "held or received" controlled trust money (or client money) and is then subject to all the rules.

(iv)   The rules do not cover money held or received by a solicitor attorney acting in a purely personal capacity outside any legal practice. If a solicitor is charging for the work, it is clearly being done in the course of legal practice. See rule 4, note (iv) for the choices which can be made on retirement from private practice.

(v)   "A client's own account" covers all accounts in a client's own name, whether opened by the client himself or herself, or by the solicitor on the client's instructions under rule 16(1)(b).

(vi)   "A client's own account" also includes an account opened in the name of a person designated by the client under rule 16(1)(b).

(vii)   Solicitors should also remember the requirements of rule 32(8) – bills and notifications of costs.

(viii)   For payment of interest, see rule 24, note (iii).

Rule 12 – Solicitor's rights not affected

Nothing in these rules deprives a *solicitor* of any recourse or right, whether by way of lien, set off, counterclaim, charge or otherwise, against money standing to the credit of a *client account*.

Rule 13 – Categories of money

All money held or received in the course of practice falls into one of the following categories:

   (a)   "client money" – money held or received for a *client*, and all other money which is not *controlled trust money* or *office money*;

(b)   "controlled trust money" – money held or received for a *controlled trust*; or

(c)   "office money" – money which belongs to the *solicitor* or the practice.

Notes

(i)   "Client money" includes money held or received:

    (a)   as agent, bailee, stakeholder, or as the donee of a power of attorney, or as a liquidator, trustee in bankruptcy or Court of Protection receiver;

    (b)   for payment of unpaid professional disbursements (for definition of "professional disbursement" see rule 2(2)(s));

    (c)   for payment of stamp duty, Land Registry registration fees, telegraphic transfer fees and court fees; this is not office money because the solicitor has not incurred an obligation to the Inland Revenue, the Land Registry, the bank or the court to pay the duty or fee (contrast with note (xi)(c)(C) below); (on the other hand, if the solicitor has already paid the duty or fee out of his or her own resources, or has received the service on credit, payment subsequently received from the client will be office money – see note (xi)(c)(B) below);

    (d)   as a payment on account of costs generally;

    (e)   as commission paid in respect of a solicitor's client, unless the client has given the solicitor prior authority to retain it in accordance with practice rule 10, or unless it falls within the £20 de minimis figure specified in that rule.

(ii)   A solicitor to whom a cheque or draft is made out, and who in the course of practice endorses it over to a client or employer, has received client money. Even if no other client money is held or received, the solicitor will be subject to some provisions of the rules, e.g.:

    ►   rule 7 (duty to remedy breaches);

    ►   rule 32 (accounting records for client money);

    ►   rule 34 (production of records);

    ►   rule 35 (delivery of accountants' reports).

(iii)   Money held by solicitors who are trustees of occupational pension schemes will either be client money or controlled trust money, according to the circumstances.

(iv)   Money held jointly with another person outside the practice (for example, with a lay trustee, or with another firm of solicitors) is client money subject to a limited application of the rules – see rule 10.

(v)   Money held to the sender's order is client money.

    (a)   If money is accepted on such terms, it must be held in a client account.

    (b)   However, a cheque or draft sent to a solicitor on terms that the cheque or draft (as opposed to the money) is held to the sender's order must not be presented for payment without the sender's consent.

    (c)   The recipient is always subject to a professional obligation to return the money, or the cheque or draft, to the sender on demand.

(vi)   An advance to a client from the solicitor which is paid into a client account under rule 15(2)(b) becomes client money. For interest, see rule 24(3)(e).

(vii)   Money subject to a trust will be either:

    (a)   controlled trust money (basically if members of the practice are the only trustees, but see the detailed definition of "controlled trust" in rule 2(2)(h)); or

    (b)   client money (if the trust is not a controlled trust; typically the solicitor will be co-trustee with a lay person, or is acting for lay trustees).

(viii) If the Office for the Supervision of Solicitors (OSS) intervenes in a practice, money from the practice is held or received by the OSS's intervention agent subject to a trust under Schedule 1 paragraph 7(1) of the Solicitors Act 1974, and is therefore controlled trust money. The same provision requires the agent to pay the money into a client account.

(ix)   A solicitor who, as the donee of a power of attorney, operates the donor's own account is subject to a limited application of these rules – see rule 11. Money kept in the donor's own account is not "client money", because it is not "held or received" by the solicitor.

(x)   Money held or received by a solicitor in the course of his or her employment when practising in one of the capacities listed in rule 5 (persons exempt from the rules) is not "client money" for the purpose of the rules, because the rules do not apply at all.

(xi)   Office money includes:

  (a) money held or received in connection with running the practice; for example, PAYE, or VAT on the firm's fees;

  (b) interest on general client accounts; the bank or building society should be instructed to credit such interest to the office account – but see also rule 15(2)(d), and note (vi) to rule 15 for interest on controlled trust money; and

  (c) payments received in respect of:

    (A) fees due to the practice against a bill or written notification of costs incurred, which has been given or sent in accordance with rule 19(2);

    (B) disbursements already paid by the practice (for definition of "disbursement" see rule 2(2)(k));

    (C) disbursements incurred but not yet paid by the practice, but excluding unpaid professional disbursements (for definition of "professional disbursement" see rule 2(2)(s), and note (v) to rule 2);

    (D) money paid for or towards an agreed fee – see rule 19(5); and

  (d) money held in a client account and earmarked for costs under rule 19(3) (transfer of costs from client account to office account); and

  (e) money held or received from the Legal Services Commission as a regular payment (see rule 21(2)).

(xii) A solicitor cannot be his or her own client for the purpose of the rules, so that if a practice conducts a personal or office transaction – for instance, conveyancing – for a principal (or for a number of principals), money held or received on behalf of the principal(s) is office money. However, other circumstances may mean that the money is client money, for example:

  (a) If the practice also acts for a lender, money held or received on behalf of the lender is client money.

  (b) If the practice acts for a principal and, for example, his or her spouse jointly (assuming the spouse is not a partner in the practice), money received on their joint behalf is client money.

  (c) If the practice acts for an assistant solicitor, consultant or non-solicitor employee, or (if it is a company) a director, or (if it is a limited liability partnership) a member, he or she is regarded as a client of the practice, and money received for him or her is client money – even if he or she conducts the matter personally.

  (d) See also note (iva) to rule 2 (money held on behalf of trustees who are head office partners of a registered European lawyer is client money).

(xiii) For a flowchart summarising the effect of the rules, see Appendix 1. For more details of the treatment of different types of money, see the chart "Special situations – what applies" at Appendix 2. These two appendices are included to help solicitors and their staff find their way about the rules. Unlike the notes, they are not intended to affect the meaning of the rules.

PART B – CLIENT MONEY, CONTROLLED TRUST MONEY AND OPERATION OF A CLIENT ACCOUNT

Rule 14 – Client accounts

(1)   A *solicitor* who holds or receives *client money* and/or *controlled trust money* must keep one or more *client accounts* (unless all the *client money* and *controlled trust money* is always dealt with outside any *client account* in accordance with rule 9, rule 10 or rules 16 to 18).

(2)   A "client account" is an account of a practice kept at a *bank* or *building society* for holding *client money* and/or *controlled trust money*, in accordance with the requirements of this part of the rules.

(3)   The *client account(s)* of:

    (a)   a sole practitioner must be either in the *solicitor's* own name or in the practice name;

    (b)   a *partnership* must be in the firm name;

    (c)   a *recognised body* must be in the company name, or the name of the limited liability partnership;

    (d)   in-house *solicitors* must be in the name of the current *principal solicitor* or *solicitors*;

    (e)   executors or *trustees* who are *controlled trustees* must be either in the name of the firm or in the name of the *controlled trustee(s)*;

and the name of the account must also include the word "client".

(4)   A *client account* must be:

    (a)   a *bank* account at a branch (or a *bank's* head office) in England and Wales; or

    (b)   a *building society* deposit or share account at a branch (or a society's head office) in England and Wales.

(5)   There are two types of *client account*:

    (a)   a "separate designated client account", which is a deposit or share account for money relating to a single *client*, or a current, deposit or share account for money held for a single *controlled trust*; and which includes in its title, in addition to the requirements of rule 14(3) above, a reference to the identity of the *client* or *controlled trust*; and

    (b)   a "general client account", which is any other *client account*.

Notes

(i)   For the client accounts of an executor, trustee or nominee company owned by a solicitor's practice, see rule 31.

(ii)   In the case of in-house solicitors, any client account should be in the names of all solicitors held out on the notepaper as principals. The names of other solicitor employees may also be included if so desired. Any solicitor whose name is included will be subject to the full Compensation Fund contribution and his or her name will have to be included on the accountant's report.

(iii)   "Bank" and "building society" are defined in rule 2(2)(c) and (d) respectively.

(iv)   A practice may have any number of separate designated client accounts and general client accounts.

(v)   The word "client" must appear in full; an abbreviation is not acceptable.

(vi)   Compliance with rule 14(1) to (4) ensures that clients, as well as the bank or building society, have the protection afforded by section 85 of the Solicitors Act 1974.

(vii)   Money held in a client account must be immediately available, even at the sacrifice of interest, unless the client otherwise instructs, or the circumstances clearly indicate otherwise.

Rule 15 – Use of a client account

(1)   *Client money* and *controlled trust money* must *without delay* be paid into a *client account*, and must be held in a *client account*, except when the rules provide to the contrary (see rules 16 to 18).

(2)   Only *client money* or *controlled trust money* may be paid into or held in a *client account*, except:

(a)   an amount of the *solicitor's* own money required to open or maintain the account;

(b)   an advance from the *solicitor* to fund a payment on behalf of a *client* or *controlled trust* in excess of funds held for that *client* or *controlled trust*; the sum becomes *client money* or *controlled trust money* on payment into the account (for interest on *client money*, see rule 24(3)(e); for interest on *controlled trust money*, see rule 24(7) and note (x) to rule 24);

(c)   money to replace any sum which for any reason has been drawn from the account in breach of rule 22; the replacement money becomes *client money* or *controlled trust money* on payment into the account; and

(d)   a sum in lieu of interest which is paid into a *client account* for the purpose of complying with rule 24(2) as an alternative to paying it to the client direct; (for interest on *controlled trust money*, see note (vi) below);

and except when the rules provide to the contrary (see note (iv) below).

Notes

(i)   See rule 13 and notes for the definition and examples of client money and controlled trust money.

(ii)   "Without delay" is defined in rule 2(2)(z).

(iii)   Exceptions to rule 15(1) (client money and controlled trust money must be paid into a client account) can be found in:

▶   rule 9 – liquidators, trustees in bankruptcy, Court of Protection receivers and trustees of occupational pension schemes;

▶   rule 10 – joint accounts;

▶   rule 16 – client's instructions;

▶   rules 17 and 18:

– cash paid straight to client, beneficiary or third party;

– cheque endorsed to client, beneficiary or third party;

– money withheld from client account on the Society's authority;

– controlled trust money paid into an account which is not a client account;

▶   rule 19(1)(b) – receipt and transfer of costs;

▶   rule 21(1) – payments by the Legal Services Commission.

(iv)   Rule 15(2)(a) to (d) provides for exceptions to the principle that only client money and controlled trust money may be paid into a client account. Additional exceptions can be found in:

►   rule 19(1)(c) – receipt and transfer of costs;

►   rule 20(2)(b) – receipt of mixed payments;

►   rule 21(2)(c)(ii) – transfer to client account of a sum for unpaid professional disbursements, where the solicitor receives regular payments from the Legal Services Commission.

(v)   Only a nominal sum will be required to open or maintain an account. In practice, banks will usually open (and, if instructed, keep open) accounts with nil balances.

(vi)   Rule 15 allows controlled trust money to be mixed with client money in a general client account. However, the general law requires a solicitor to act in the best interests of a controlled trust and not to benefit from it. The interest rules in Part C do not apply to controlled trust money. A solicitor's legal duty means that the solicitor must obtain the best reasonably obtainable rate of interest, and must account to the relevant controlled trust for all the interest earned, whether the controlled trust money is held in a separate designated client account or in a general client account. To ensure that all interest is accounted for, one option might be to set up a general client account just for controlled trust money. When controlled trust money is held in a general client account, interest will be credited to the office account in the normal way, but all interest must be promptly allocated to each controlled trust – either by transfer to the general client account, or to separate designated client account(s) for the particular trust(s), or by payment to each trust in some other way.

Solicitors should also consider whether they have received any indirect benefit from controlled trust money at the expense of the controlled trust(s). For example, the bank might charge a reduced overdraft rate by reference to the total funds (including controlled trust money) held, in return for paying a lower rate of interest on those funds. In this type of case, the law may require the solicitor to do more than simply account for any interest earned.

(vii)   If controlled trust money is invested in the purchase of assets other than money – such as stocks or shares – it ceases to be controlled trust money, because it is no longer money held by the solicitor. If the investment is subsequently sold, the money received is, again, controlled trust money. The records kept under rule 32 must include entries to show the purchase or sale of investments.

(viii)   Some schemes proposed by banks would aggregate the sums held in a number of client accounts in order to maximise the interest payable. It is not acceptable to aggregate money held in separate designated client accounts with money held in general client accounts (see note (i) to rule 24).

(ix)   In the case of *Wood and Burdett* (case number 8669/2002 filed on 13th January 2004), the Solicitors' Disciplinary Tribunal said that it is not a proper part of a solicitor's everyday business or practice to operate a banking facility for third parties, whether they are clients of the firm or not. Solicitors should not, therefore, provide banking facilities through a client account. Further, solicitors are likely to lose the exemption under the Financial Services and Markets Act 2000 if a deposit is taken in circumstances which do not form part of a solicitor's practice. It should also be borne in mind that there are criminal sanctions against assisting money launderers.

Rule 16 – Client money withheld from client account on client's instructions

(1)   *Client money* may be:

(a)   held by the *solicitor* outside a *client account* by, for example, retaining it in the *solicitor's* safe in the form of cash, or placing it in an account in the *solicitor's* name which is not a *client account*, such as an account outside England and Wales; or

    (b)   paid into an account at a *bank*, *building society* or other financial institution opened in the name of the *client* or of a person designated by the *client*;

but only if the *client* instructs the *solicitor* to that effect for the *client's* own convenience, and only if the instructions are given in writing, or are given by other means and confirmed by the *solicitor* to the *client* in writing.

(2)   It is improper to seek blanket agreements, through standard terms of business or otherwise, to hold *client money* outside a *client account*.

Notes

(i)   For advance payments from the Legal Services Commission, withheld from a client account on the Commission's instructions, see rule 21(1)(a).

(ii)   If a client instructs the solicitor to hold part only of a payment in accordance with rule 16(1)(a) or (b), the entire payment must first be placed in a client account. The relevant part can then be transferred out and dealt with in accordance with the client's instructions.

(iii)   Money withheld from a client account under rule 16(1)(a) remains client money, and the record-keeping provisions of rule 32 must be complied with.

(iv)   Once money has been paid into an account set up under rule 16(1)(b), it ceases to be client money. Until that time, the money is client money and a record must therefore be kept of the solicitor's receipt of the money, and its payment into the account in the name of the client or designated person, in accordance with rule 32. If the solicitor can operate the account, the solicitor must comply with rule 11 (operating a client's own account) and rule 33 (accounting records for clients' own accounts). In the absence of instructions to the contrary, any money withdrawn must be paid into a client account – see rule 15(1).

(v)   Clients' instructions under rule 16(1) must be kept for at least six years – see rule 32(9)(d).

(vi)   A payment on account of costs received from a person who is funding all or part of the solicitor's fees may be withheld from a client account on the instructions of that person given in accordance with rule 16(1) and (2).

(vii)   For payment of interest, see rule 24(6) and notes (ii) and (iii) to rule 24.

Rule 17 – Other client money withheld from a client account

The following categories of *client money* may be withheld from a *client account*:

    (a)   cash received and *without delay* paid in cash in the ordinary course of business to the *client* or, on the *client's* behalf, to a third party;

    (b)   a cheque or draft received and endorsed over in the ordinary course of business to the *client* or, on the *client's* behalf, to a third party;

    (c)   money withheld from a *client account* on instructions under rule 16;

    (d)   unpaid *professional disbursements* included in a payment of *costs* dealt with under rule 19(1)(b);

    (e)   (i)   advance payments from the Legal Services Commission withheld from *client account* (see rule 21(1)(a)); and

          (ii)   unpaid *professional disbursements* included in a payment of *costs* from the Legal Services Commission (see rule 21(1)(b)); and

(f)   money withheld from a *client account* on the written authorisation of the *Society*. The *Society* may impose a condition that the *solicitor* pay the money to a charity which gives an indemnity against any legitimate claim subsequently made for the sum received.

Notes

(i)   "Without delay" is defined in rule 2(2)(z).

(ii)   If money is withheld from a client account under rule 17(a) or (b), rule 32 requires records to be kept of the receipt of the money and the payment out.

(iii)   It makes no difference, for the purpose of the rules, whether an endorsement is effected by signature in the normal way or by some other arrangement with the bank.

(iv)   The circumstances in which authorisation would be given under rule 17(f) must be extremely rare. Applications for authorisation should be made to the Professional Ethics Division.

Rule 18 – Controlled trust money withheld from a client account

The following categories of *controlled trust money* may be withheld from a *client account*:

(a)   cash received and *without delay* paid in cash in the execution of the *trust* to a beneficiary or third party;

(b)   a cheque or draft received and *without delay* endorsed over in the execution of the *trust* to a beneficiary or third party;

(c)   money which, in accordance with the *trustee's* powers, is paid into or retained in an account of the *trustee* which is not a *client account* (for example, an account outside England and Wales), or properly retained in cash in the performance of the *trustee's* duties;

(d)   money withheld from a *client account* on the written authorisation of the *Society*. The *Society* may impose a condition that the *solicitor* pay the money to a charity which gives an indemnity against any legitimate claim subsequently made for the sum received.

Notes

(i)   "Without delay" is defined in rule 2(2)(z).

(ii)   If money is withheld from a client account under rule 18(a) or (b), rule 32 requires records to be kept of the receipt of the money and the payment out – see also rule 15, note (vii). If money is withheld from a client account under rule 18(c), rule 32 requires a record to be kept of the receipt of the money.

(iii)   It makes no difference, for the purpose of the rules, whether an endorsement is effected by signature in the normal way or by some other arrangement with the bank.

(iv)   The circumstances in which authorisation would be given under rule 18(d) must be extremely rare. Applications for authorisation should be made to the Professional Ethics Division.

Rule 19 – Receipt and transfer of costs

(1)   A *solicitor* who receives money paid in full or part settlement of the *solicitor's* bill (or other notification of *costs*) **must follow one of the following four options:**

(a)   **determine the composition of the payment *without delay*, and deal with the money accordingly:**

    (i)   if the sum comprises *office money* only, it must be placed in an *office account*;

    (ii)   if the sum comprises only *client money* (for example an unpaid *professional disbursement* – see rule 2(2)(s), and note (v) to rule 2), the entire sum must be placed in a *client account*;

    (iii)   if the sum includes both *office money* and *client money* (such as unpaid *professional disbursements*; purchase money; or payments in advance for court fees, stamp duty, Land Registry registration fees or telegraphic transfer fees), the *solicitor* must follow rule 20 (receipt of mixed payments); **or**

(b)   **ascertain that the payment comprises only *office money*, and/or *client money* in the form of *professional disbursements* incurred but not yet paid, and deal with the payment as follows:**

    (i)   place the entire sum in an *office account* at a *bank* or *building society* branch (or head office) in England and Wales; and

    (ii)   by the end of the second working day following receipt, either pay any unpaid *professional disbursement*, or transfer a sum for its settlement to a *client account*; **or**

(c)   **pay the entire sum into a *client account* (regardless of its composition), and transfer any *office money* out of the *client account* within 14 days of receipt; or**

(d)   **on receipt of *costs* from the Legal Services Commission, follow the option in rule 21(1)(b).**

(2)   A *solicitor* who properly requires payment of his or her *fees* from money held for the *client* or *controlled trust* in a *client account* must first give or send a bill of *costs*, or other written notification of the *costs* incurred, to the *client* or the paying party.

(3)   Once the *solicitor* has complied with paragraph (2) above, the money earmarked for costs becomes *office money* and must be transferred out of the *client account* within 14 days.

(4)   A payment on account of *costs* generally is *client money*, and must be held in a *client account* until the *solicitor* has complied with paragraph (2) above. (For an exception in the case of legal aid payments, see rule 21(1)(a).)

(5)   A payment for an *agreed fee* must be paid into an *office account*. An "agreed fee" is one that is fixed – not a *fee* that can be varied upwards, nor a *fee* that is dependent on the transaction being completed. An *agreed fee* must be evidenced in writing.

Notes

(i)   For the definition and further examples of office and client money, see rule 13 and notes.

(ii)   ▶   Money received for paid disbursements is office money.

    ▶   Money received for unpaid professional disbursements is client money.

    ▶   Money received for other unpaid disbursements for which the solicitor has incurred a liability to the payee (for example, travel agents' charges, taxi fares, courier charges or Land Registry search fees, payable on credit) is office money.

▶   Money received for disbursements anticipated but not yet incurred is a payment on account, and is therefore client money.

(iii)   The option in rule 19(1)(a) allows a solicitor to place all payments in the correct account in the first instance. The option in rule 19(1)(b) allows the prompt banking into an office account of an invoice payment when the only uncertainty is whether or not the payment includes some client money in the form of unpaid professional disbursements. The option in rule 19(1)(c) allows the prompt banking into a client account of any invoice payment in advance of determining whether the payment is a mixture of office and client money (of whatever description) or is only office money.

(iv)   A solicitor who is not in a position to comply with the requirements of rule 19(1)(b) cannot take advantage of that option.

(v)   The option in rule 19(1)(b) cannot be used if the money received includes a payment on account – for example, a payment for a professional disbursement anticipated but not yet incurred.

(vi)   In order to be able to use the option in rule 19(1)(b) for electronic payments or other direct transfers from clients, a solicitor may choose to establish a system whereby clients are given an office account number for payment of costs. The system must be capable of ensuring that, when invoices are sent to the client, no request is made for any client money, with the sole exception of money for professional disbursements already incurred but not yet paid.

(vii)   Rule 19(1)(c) allows clients to be given a single account number for making direct payments by electronic or other means – under this option, it has to be a client account.

(viii)   A solicitor will not be in breach of rule 19 as a result of a misdirected electronic payment or other direct transfer, provided:

(A)   appropriate systems are in place to ensure compliance;

(B)   appropriate instructions were given to the client;

(C)   the client's mistake is remedied promptly upon discovery; and

(D)   appropriate steps are taken to avoid future errors by the client.

(ix)   "Properly" in rule 19(2) implies that the work has actually been done, whether at the end of the matter or at an interim stage, and that the solicitor is entitled to appropriate the money for costs.

(x)   Costs transferred out of a client account in accordance with rule 19(2) and (3) must be specific sums relating to the bill or other written notification of costs, and covered by the amount held for the particular client or controlled trust. Round sum withdrawals on account of costs will be a breach of the rules.

(xi)   In the case of a controlled trust, the paying party will be the controlled trustee(s) themselves. The solicitor must keep the original bill or notification of costs on the file, in addition to complying with rule 32(8) (central record or file of copy bills, etc.).

(xii)   Undrawn costs must not remain in a client account as a "cushion" against any future errors which could result in a shortage on that account, and cannot be regarded as available to set off against any general shortage on client account.

(xiii)   The rules do not require a bill of costs for an agreed fee, although a solicitor's VAT position may mean that in practice a bill is needed. If there is no bill, the written evidence of the agreement must be filed as a written notification of costs under rule 32(8)(b).

Rule 20 – Receipt of mixed payments

(1)   A "mixed payment" is one which includes *client money* or *controlled trust money* as well as *office money*.

(2)   A *mixed payment* must either:

    (a)   be split between a *client account* and *office account* as appropriate; or

    (b)   be placed *without delay* in a *client account*.

(3)   If the entire payment is placed in a *client account*, all *office money* must be transferred out of the *client account* within 14 days of receipt.

(4)   See rule 19(1)(b) and (c) for additional ways of dealing with (among other things) *mixed payments* received in response to a bill or other notification of *costs*.

(5)   See rule 21(1)(b) for (among other things) *mixed payments* received from the Legal Services Commission.

Note

"Without delay" is defined in rule 2(2)(z).

Rule 21 – Treatment of payments to legal aid practitioners

Payments from the Legal Services Commission

(1)   Two special dispensations apply to payments (other than regular payments) from the Legal Services Commission:

    (a)   An advance payment in anticipation of work to be carried out, although *client money*, may be placed in an *office account*, provided the commission instructs in writing that this may be done.

    (b)   A payment for *costs* (interim and/or final) may be paid into an *office account* at a *bank* or *building society* branch (or head office) in England and Wales, regardless of whether it consists wholly of *office money*, or is mixed with *client money* in the form of:

        (i)   advance payments for *fees* or *disbursements*; or

        (ii)   money for unpaid *professional disbursements*;

        provided all money for payment of *disbursements* is transferred to a *client account* (or the *disbursements* paid) within 14 days of receipt.

(2)   The following provisions apply to *regular payments* from the Legal Services Commission:

    (a)   "Regular payments" (which are *office money*) are:

        (i)   standard monthly payments paid by the Commission under the civil legal aid contracting arrangements;

        (ii)   monthly payments paid by the Commission under the criminal legal aid contracting arrangements; and

        (iii)   any other payments for work done or to be done received from the Commission under an arrangement for payments on a regular basis.

    (b)   *Regular payments* must be paid into an *office account* at a *bank* or *building society* branch (or head office) in England and Wales.

(c)　A *solicitor* must within 28 days of submitting a report to the Commission, notifying completion of a matter, either:

(i)　pay any unpaid *professional disbursement(s)*, or

(ii)　transfer to a *client account* a sum equivalent to the amount of any unpaid *professional disbursement(s)*,

relating to that matter.

(d)　In cases where the Commission permits solicitors to submit reports at various stages during a matter rather than only at the end of a matter, the requirement in paragraph (c) above applies to any unpaid *professional disbursement(s)* included in each report so submitted.

Payments from a third party

(3)　If the Legal Services Commission has paid any costs to a *solicitor* or a previously nominated *solicitor* in a matter (advice and assistance or legal help *costs*, advance payments or interim *costs*), or has paid *professional disbursements* direct, and *costs* are subsequently settled by a third party:

(a)　The entire third party payment must be paid into a *client account*.

(b)　A sum representing the payments made by the Commission must be retained in the *client account*.

(c)　Any balance belonging to the *solicitor* must be transferred to an *office account* within 14 days of the *solicitor* sending a report to the Commission containing details of the third party payment.

(d)　The sum retained in the *client account* as representing payments made by the Commission must be:

(i)　**either** recorded in the individual *client's* ledger account, and identified as the Commission's money;

(ii)　**or** recorded in a ledger account in the Commission's name, and identified by reference to the *client* or matter;

and kept in the *client account* until notification from the Commission that it has recouped an equivalent sum from subsequent payments due to the *solicitor*. The retained sum must be transferred to an *office account* within 14 days of notification.

Notes

(i)　This rule deals with matters which specifically affect legal aid practitioners. It should not be read in isolation from the remainder of the rules which apply to all solicitors, including legal aid practitioners.

(ii)　Franchised firms can apply for advance payments on the issue of a certificate. The Legal Services Commission has issued instructions that these payments may be placed in office account. For regular payments, see notes (vii)–(x) below.

(iii)　Rule 21(1)(b) deals with the specific problems of legal aid practitioners by allowing a mixed or indeterminate payment of costs (or even a payment consisting entirely of unpaid professional disbursements) to be paid into an office account, which for the purpose of rule 21(1)(b) must be an account at a bank or building society. However, it is always open to the solicitor to comply with rule 19(1)(a) to (c), which are the options for all solicitors for the receipt of costs. For regular payments, see notes (vii)–(x) below.

(iv)   Solicitors are required by the Legal Services Commission to report promptly to the Commission on receipt of costs from a third party. It is advisable to keep a copy of the report on the file as proof of compliance with the Commission's requirements, as well as to demonstrate compliance with the rule.

(v)   A third party payment may also include unpaid professional disbursements or outstanding costs of the client's previous solicitor. This part of the payment is client money and must be kept in a client account until the solicitor pays the professional disbursement or outstanding costs.

(vi)   In rule 21, and elsewhere in the rules, references to the Legal Services Commission are to be read, where appropriate, as including the Legal Aid Board.

(vii)   Regular payments are office money and are defined as such in the rules (rule 13, note (xi)(e)). They are neither advance payments nor payments of costs for the purposes of the rules. Regular payments must be paid into an office account which for the purpose of rule 21(2)(b) must be an account at a bank or building society.

(viii)   Firms in receipt of regular payments must deal with unpaid professional disbursements in the way prescribed by rule 21(2)(c). The rule permits a solicitor who is required to transfer an amount to cover unpaid professional disbursements into a client account to make the transfer from his or her own resources if the regular payments are insufficient.

(ix)   The 28 day time limit for paying, or transferring an amount to a client account for, unpaid professional disbursements is for the purposes of these rules only. An earlier deadline may be imposed by contract with the Commission or with counsel, agents or experts. On the other hand, a solicitor may have agreed to pay later than 28 days from the submission of the report notifying completion of a matter, in which case rule 21(2)(c) will require a transfer of the appropriate amount to a client account (but not payment) within 28 days. Solicitors are reminded of their professional obligation to pay the fees of counsel, agents and experts.

(x)   For the appropriate accounting records for regular payments, see note (v) to rule 32.

Rule 22 – Withdrawals from a client account

(1)   *Client money* may only be withdrawn from a *client account* when it is:

(a)   properly required for a payment to or on behalf of the *client* (or other person on whose behalf the money is being held);

(b)   properly required for payment of a *disbursement* on behalf of the *client*;

(c)   properly required in full or partial reimbursement of money spent by the *solicitor* on behalf of the *client*;

(d)   transferred to another *client account*;

(e)   withdrawn on the *client's* instructions, provided the instructions are for the *client's* convenience and are given in writing, or are given by other means and confirmed by the *solicitor* to the *client* in writing;

(f)   a refund to the *solicitor* of an advance no longer required to fund a payment on behalf of a *client* (see rule 15(2)(b));

(g)   money which has been paid into the account in breach of the rules (for example, money paid into the wrong *separate designated client account*) – see paragraph (4) below; or

(h)   money not covered by (a) to (g) above, withdrawn from the account on the written authorisation of the *Society*. The *Society* may impose a condition that the *solicitor* pay the money to a charity which gives an indemnity against any legitimate claim subsequently made for the sum received.

(2) *Controlled trust money* may only be withdrawn from a *client account* when it is:

(a) properly required for a payment in the execution of the particular *trust*, including the purchase of an investment (other than money) in accordance with the *trustee's* powers;

(b) properly required for payment of a *disbursement* for the particular *trust*;

(c) properly required in full or partial reimbursement of money spent by the *solicitor* on behalf of the particular *trust*;

(d) transferred to another *client account*;

(e) transferred to an account other than a *client account* (such as an account outside England and Wales), but only if the *trustee's* powers permit, or to be properly retained in cash in the performance of the *trustee's* duties;

(f) a refund to the *solicitor* of an advance no longer required to fund a payment on behalf of a *controlled trust* (see rule 15(2)(b));

(g) money which has been paid into the account in breach of the rules (for example, money paid into the wrong *separate designated client account*) – see paragraph (4) below; or

(h) money not covered by (a) to (g) above, withdrawn from the account on the written authorisation of the *Society*. The *Society* may impose a condition that the *solicitor* pay the money to a charity which gives an indemnity against any legitimate claim subsequently made for the sum received.

(3) *Office money* may only be withdrawn from a *client account* when it is:

(a) money properly paid into the account to open or maintain it under rule 15(2)(a);

(b) properly required for payment of the *solicitor's costs* under rule 19(2) and (3);

(c) the whole or part of a payment into a *client account* under rule 19(1)(c);

(d) part of a *mixed payment* placed in a *client account* under rule 20(2)(b); or

(e) money which has been paid into a *client account* in breach of the rules (for example, interest wrongly credited to a *general client account*) – see paragraph (4) below.

(4) Money which has been paid into a *client account* in breach of the rules must be withdrawn from the *client account* promptly upon discovery.

(5) Money withdrawn in relation to a particular *client* or *controlled trust* from a *general client account* must not exceed the money held on behalf of that *client* or *controlled trust* in all the *solicitor's general client accounts* (except as provided in paragraph (6) below).

(6) A *solicitor* may make a payment in respect of a particular *client* or *controlled trust* out of a *general client account*, even if no money (or insufficient money) is held for that *client* or *controlled trust* in the *solicitor's general client account(s)*, provided:

(a) sufficient money is held for that *client* or *controlled trust* in a *separate designated client account*; and

(b) the appropriate transfer from the *separate designated client account* to a *general client account* is made immediately.

(7) Money held for a *client* or *controlled trust* in a *separate designated client account* must not be used for payments for another *client* or *controlled trust*.

(8)   A *client account* must not be overdrawn, except in the following circumstances:

  (a)   A *separate designated client account* for a *controlled trust* can be overdrawn if the *controlled trustee* makes payments on behalf of the *trust* (for example, inheritance tax) before realising sufficient assets to cover the payments.

  (b)   If a sole practitioner dies and his or her *client accounts* are frozen, the *solicitor*-manager can operate *client accounts* which are overdrawn to the extent of the money held in the frozen accounts.

Notes

Withdrawals in favour of solicitor, and for payment of disbursements

(i)   Disbursements to be paid direct from a client account, or already paid out of the solicitor's own money, can be withdrawn under rule 22(1)(b) or (c) (or rule 22(2)(b) or (c)) in advance of preparing a bill of costs. Money to be withdrawn from a client account for the payment of costs (fees and disbursements) under rule 19(2) and (3) becomes office money and is dealt with under rule 22(3)(b).

(ii)   Money is "spent" under rule 22(1)(c) (or rule 22(2)(c)) at the time when the solicitor despatches a cheque, unless the cheque is to be held to the solicitor's order. Money is also regarded as "spent" by the use of a credit account, so that, for example, search fees, taxi fares and courier charges incurred in this way may be transferred to the solicitor's office account.

(iii)   See rule 23(3) for the way in which a withdrawal from a client account in favour of the solicitor must be effected.

Cheques payable to banks, building societies, etc.

(iv)   In order to protect clients' funds (or controlled trust funds) against misappropriation when cheques are made payable to banks, building societies or other large institutions, it is strongly recommended that solicitors add the name and number of the account after the payee's name.

Drawing against uncleared cheques

(v)   A solicitor should use discretion in drawing against a cheque received from or on behalf of a client before it has been cleared. If the cheque is not met, other clients' money will have been used to make the payment in breach of the rules. See rule 7 (duty to remedy breaches). A solicitor may be able to avoid a breach of the rules by instructing the bank or building society to charge all unpaid credits to the solicitor's office or personal account.

Non-receipt of telegraphic transfer

(vi)   If a solicitor acting for a client withdraws money from a general client account on the strength of information that a telegraphic transfer is on its way, but the telegraphic transfer does not arrive, the solicitor will have used other clients' money in breach of the rules. See also rule 7 (duty to remedy breaches).

Withdrawals on instructions

(vii)   One of the reasons why a client might authorise a withdrawal under rule 22(1)(e) might be to have the money transferred to a type of account other than a client account. If so, the requirements of rule 16 must be complied with.

Withdrawals on the Society's authorisation

(viii) Applications for authorisation under rule 22(1)(h) or 22(2)(h) should be made to the Professional Ethics Division, who can advise on the criteria which must normally be met for authorisation to be given.

(ix) After a practice has been wound up, banks sometimes discover unclaimed balances in an old client account. This money remains subject to rule 22 and rule 23. An application can be made to the Society under rule 22(1)(h) or 22(2)(h).

Rule 23 – Method of and authority for withdrawals from client account

(1) A withdrawal from a *client account* may be made only after a specific authority in respect of that withdrawal has been signed by at least one of the following:

(a) a *solicitor* who holds a current practising certificate or a *registered European lawyer*;

(b) a Fellow of the Institute of Legal Executives of at least three years standing who is employed by such a *solicitor*, a *registered European lawyer* or a *recognised body*;

(c) in the case of an office dealing solely with conveyancing, a licensed conveyancer who is employed by such a *solicitor*, a *registered European lawyer* or a *recognised body*; or

(d) a *registered foreign lawyer* who is a *partner* in the practice, or who is a director of the practice (if it is a company), or who is a member of the practice (if it is a limited liability partnership).

(2) There is no need to comply with paragraph (1) above when transferring money from one *general client account* to another *general client account* at the same *bank* or *building society*.

(3) A withdrawal from a *client account* in favour of the *solicitor* or the practice must be either by way of a cheque to the *solicitor* or practice, or by way of a transfer to the *office account* or to the *solicitor's* personal account. The withdrawal must not be made in cash.

Notes

(i) Instructions to the bank or building society to withdraw money from a client account (rule 23(1)) may be given over the telephone, provided a specific authority has been signed in accordance with this rule before the instructions are given. If a solicitor decides to take advantage of this arrangement, it is of paramount importance that the scheme has appropriate inbuilt safeguards, such as passwords, to give the greatest protection possible for client money (or controlled trust money). Suitable safeguards will also be needed for practices which operate a CHAPS terminal.

(ii) In the case of a withdrawal by cheque, the specific authority (rule 23(1)) is usually a signature on the cheque itself. Signing a blank cheque is not a specific authority.

(iii) A withdrawal from a client account by way of a private loan from one client to another can only be made if the provisions of rule 30(2) are complied with.

(iv) It is advisable that a withdrawal for payment to or on behalf of a client (or on behalf of a controlled trust) be made by way of a crossed cheque whenever possible.

(v) Controlled trustees who instruct an outside manager to run, or continue to run, on a day-to-day basis, the business or property portfolio of an estate or trust will not need to comply with rule 23(1), provided all cheques are retained in accordance with rule 32(10). (See also rule 32, note (ii)(d).)

(vi)   Where the sum due to the client is sufficiently large, the solicitor should consider whether it should not appropriately be transferred to the client by direct bank transfer. For doing this, the solicitor would be entitled to make a modest administrative charge in addition to any charge made by the bank in connection with the transfer.

PART C – INTEREST

Rule 24 – When interest must be paid

(1)   When a *solicitor* holds money in a *separate designated client account* for a *client*, or for a person funding all or part of the *solicitor's fees*, the *solicitor* must account to the *client* or that person for all interest earned on the account.

(2)   When a *solicitor* holds money in a *general client account* for a *client*, or for a person funding all or part of the *solicitor's fees* (or if money should have been held for a *client* or such other person in a *client account* but was not), the *solicitor* must account to the *client* or that person for a sum in lieu of interest calculated in accordance with rule 25.

(3)   A *solicitor* is not required to pay a sum in lieu of interest under paragraph (2) above:

    (a)   if the amount calculated is £20 or less;

    (b)   (i)   if the *solicitor* holds a sum of money not exceeding the amount shown in the left hand column below for a time not exceeding the period indicated in the right hand column:

Amount	Time
£1,000	8 weeks
£2,000	4 weeks
£10,000	2 weeks
£20,000	1 week

        (ii)   if the *solicitor* holds a sum of money exceeding £20,000 for one week or less, unless it is fair and reasonable to account for a sum in lieu of interest having regard to all the circumstances;

    (c)   on money held for the payment of counsel's fees, once counsel has requested a delay in settlement;

    (d)   on money held for the Legal Services Commission;

    (e)   on an advance from the *solicitor* under rule 15(2)(b) to fund a payment on behalf of the *client* in excess of funds held for that *client*; or

    (f)   if there is an agreement to contract out of the provisions of this rule under rule 27.

(4)   If sums of money are held intermittently during the course of acting, and the sum in lieu of interest calculated under rule 25 for any period is £20 or less, a sum in lieu of interest should still be paid if it is fair and reasonable in the circumstances to aggregate the sums in respect of the individual periods.

(5)   If money is held for a continuous period, and for part of that period it is held in a *separate designated client account*, the sum in lieu of interest for the rest of the period when the money was held in a *general client account* may as a result be £20 or less. A sum in lieu of interest should, however, be paid if it is fair and reasonable in the circumstances to do so.

(6) (a) If a *solicitor* holds money for a *client* (or person funding all or part of the *solicitor's fees*) in an account opened on the instructions of the *client* (or that person) under rule 16(1)(a), the *solicitor* must account to the *client* (or that person) for all interest earned on the account.

(b) If a *solicitor* has failed to comply with instructions to open an account under rule 16(1)(a), the *solicitor* must account to the *client* (or the person funding all or part of the *solicitor's fees*) for a sum in lieu of any net loss of interest suffered by the *client* (or that person) as a result.

(7) This rule does not apply to *controlled trust money*.

Notes

Requirement to pay interest

(i)　The whole of the interest earned on a separate designated client account must be credited to the account. However, the obligation to pay a sum in lieu of interest for amounts held in a general client account is subject to the de minimis provisions in rule 24(3)(a) and (b). Section 33(3) of the Solicitors Act 1974 permits solicitors to retain any interest earned on client money held in a general client account over and above that which they have to pay under these rules. (See also note (viii) to rule 15 on aggregation of accounts.)

(ii)　There is no requirement to pay a sum in lieu of interest on money held on instructions under rule 16(1)(a) in a manner which attracts no interest.

(iii)　Accounts opened in the client's name under rule 16(1)(b) (whether operated by the solicitor or not) are not subject to rule 24, as the money is not held by the solicitor. All interest earned belongs to the client. The same applies to any account in the client's own name operated by the solicitor as signatory under rule 11.

(iv)　Money subject to a trust which is not a controlled trust is client money (see rule 13, note (vii)), and rule 24 therefore applies to it.

De minimis provisions (rule 24(3)(a) and (b))

(v)　The sum in lieu of interest is calculated over the whole period for which money is held (see rule 25(2)); if this sum is £20 or less, the solicitor need not account to the client. If sums of money are held in relation to separate matters for the same client, it is normally appropriate to treat the money relating to the different matters separately, so that, if any of the sums calculated is £20 or less, no sum in lieu of interest is payable. There will, however, be cases when the matters are so closely related that they ought to be considered together – for example, when a solicitor is acting for a client in connection with numerous debt collection matters.

Administrative charges

(vi)　It is not improper to charge a reasonable fee for the handling of client money when the service provided is out of the ordinary.

Unpresented cheques

(vii)　A client may fail to present a cheque to his or her bank for payment. Whether or not it is reasonable to recalculate the amount due will depend on all the circumstances of the case. A reasonable charge may be made for any extra work carried out if the solicitor is legally entitled to make such a charge.

Liquidators, trustees in bankruptcy, Court of Protection receivers and trustees of occupational pension schemes

(viii) Under rule 9, Part C of the rules does not normally apply to solicitors who are liquidators, etc. Solicitors must comply with the appropriate statutory rules and regulations, and rules 9(3) and (4) as appropriate.

Joint accounts

(ix)   Under rule 10, Part C of the rules does not apply to joint accounts. If a solicitor holds money jointly with a client, interest earned on the account will be for the benefit of the client unless otherwise agreed. If money is held jointly with another solicitor's practice, the allocation of interest earned will depend on the agreement reached.

Requirements for controlled trust money (rule 24(7))

(x)   Part C does not apply to controlled trust money. Under the general law, trustees of a controlled trust must account for all interest earned. For the treatment of interest on controlled trust money in a general client account, see rule 13, note (xi)(b), rule 15(2)(d) and note (vi) to rule 15. (See also note (viii) to rule 15 on aggregation of accounts.)

Rule 25 – Amount of interest

(1)   *Solicitors* must aim to obtain a reasonable rate of interest on money held in a *separate designated client account*, and must account for a fair sum in lieu of interest on money held in a *general client account* (or on money which should have been held in a *client account* but was not). The sum in lieu of interest need not necessarily reflect the highest rate of interest obtainable but it is not acceptable to look only at the lowest rate of interest obtainable.

(2)   **The sum in lieu of interest** for money held in a *general client account* (or on money which should have been held in a *client account* but was not) **must be calculated**

> ► **on the balance or balances held over the whole period for which cleared funds are held**

> ► **at a rate not less than (whichever is the higher of) the following**

>> (i)   the rate of interest payable on a *separate designated client account* for the amount or amounts held, or

>> (ii)   the rate of interest payable on the relevant amount or amounts if placed on deposit on similar terms by a member of the business community

> ► **at the *bank* or *building society* where the money is held.**

(3)   If the money, or part of it, is held successively or concurrently in accounts at different *banks* or *building societies*, the relevant *bank* or *building society* for the purpose of paragraph (2) will be whichever of those *banks* or *building societies* offered the best rate on the date when the money was first held.

(4)   If, contrary to the rules, the money is not held in a *client account*, the relevant *bank* or *building society* for the purpose of paragraph (2) will be a clearing *bank* or *building society* nominated by the *client* (or other person on whose behalf *client money* is held).

Notes

(i)   The sum in lieu of interest has to be calculated over the whole period for which money is held – see rule 25(2). The solicitor will usually account to the client at the conclusion of the client's matter, but might in some cases consider it appropriate to account to the client at intervals throughout.

(ii)   When looking at the period over which the sum in lieu of interest must be calculated, it will usually be unnecessary to check on actual clearance dates. When money is received by cheque and paid out by cheque, the normal clearance periods will usually cancel each other out, so that it will be satisfactory to look at the period between the dates when the incoming cheque is banked and the outgoing cheque is drawn.

(iii)   Different considerations apply when payments in and out are not both made by cheque. So, for example, the relevant periods would normally be:

- ▶ from the date when a solicitor receives incoming money in cash until the date when the outgoing cheque is sent;

- ▶ from the date when an incoming telegraphic transfer begins to earn interest until the date when the outgoing cheque is sent;

- ▶ from the date when an incoming cheque or banker's draft is or would normally be cleared until the date when the outgoing telegraphic transfer is made or banker's draft is obtained.

(iv)   The sum in lieu of interest is calculated by reference to the rates paid by the appropriate bank or building society (see rule 25(2) to (4)). Solicitors will therefore follow the practice of that bank or building society in determining how often interest is compounded over the period for which the cleared funds are held.

(v)   Money held in a client account must be immediately available, even at the sacrifice of interest, unless the client otherwise instructs, or the circumstances clearly indicate otherwise. The need for access can be taken into account in assessing the appropriate rate for calculating the sum to be paid in lieu of interest, or in assessing whether a reasonable rate of interest has been obtained for a separate designated client account.

Rule 26 – Interest on stakeholder money

When a *solicitor* holds money as stakeholder, the *solicitor* must pay interest, or a sum in lieu of interest, on the basis set out in rule 24 to the person to whom the stake is paid.

Note

For contracting out of this provision, see rule 27(2) and the notes to rule 27.

Rule 27 – Contracting out

(1)   In appropriate circumstances a *client* and his or her *solicitor* may by a written agreement come to a different arrangement as to the matters dealt with in rule 24 (payment of interest).

(2)   A *solicitor* acting as stakeholder may, by a written agreement with his or her own *client* and the other party to the transaction, come to a different arrangement as to the matters dealt with in rule 24.

Notes

(i)   Solicitors should act fairly towards their clients and provide sufficient information to enable them to give informed consent if it is felt appropriate to depart from the interest provisions. Whether it is appropriate to contract out depends on all the circumstances, for example, the size of the sum involved or the nature or status or bargaining position of the client. It might, for instance, be appropriate to contract out by standard terms of business if the client is a substantial commercial entity and the interest involved is modest in relation to the size of the transaction. The larger the sum of interest involved, the more there would be an onus on the solicitor to show that a client who had accepted a contracting out provision was properly informed and had been treated fairly. Contracting out is never appropriate if it is against the client's interests.

(ii)   In principle, a solicitor-stakeholder is entitled to make a reasonable charge to the client for acting as stakeholder in the client's matter.

(iii)   Alternatively, it may be appropriate to include a special provision in the contract that the solicitor-stakeholder retains the interest on the deposit to cover his or her charges for acting as stakeholder. This is only acceptable if it will provide a fair and reasonable payment for the work and risk involved in holding a stake. The contract could stipulate a maximum charge, with any interest earned above that figure being paid to the recipient of the stake.

(iv)   Any right to charge the client, or to stipulate for a charge which may fall on the client, would be excluded by, for instance, a prior agreement with the client for a fixed fee for the client's matter, or for an estimated fee which cannot be varied upwards in the absence of special circumstances. It is therefore not normal practice for a stakeholder in conveyancing transactions to receive a separate payment for holding the stake.

(v)   A solicitor-stakeholder who seeks an agreement to exclude the operation of rule 26 should be particularly careful not to take unfair advantage either of the client, or of the other party if unrepresented.

Rule 28 – Interest certificates

Without prejudice to any other remedy:

(a)   any *client*, including one of joint *clients*, or a person funding all or part of a *solicitor's fees*, may apply to the *Society* for a certificate as to whether or not interest, or a sum in lieu of interest, should have been paid and, if so, the amount; and

(b)   if the *Society* certifies that interest, or a sum in lieu of interest, should have been paid, the *solicitor* must pay the certified sum.

Notes

(i)   Applications for an interest certificate should be made to the Office for the Supervision of Solicitors (OSS). It is advisable for the client (or other person) to try to resolve the matter with the solicitor before approaching the OSS.

(ii)   If appropriate, the OSS will require the solicitor to obtain an interest calculation from the relevant bank or building society.

PART D – ACCOUNTING SYSTEMS AND RECORDS

Rule 29 – Guidelines for accounting procedures and systems

The Council of the Law Society, with the concurrence of the Master of the Rolls, may from time to time publish guidelines for accounting procedures and systems to assist *solicitors* to comply with Parts A to D of the rules, and *solicitors* may be required to justify any departure from the guidelines.

Notes

(i) The current guidelines appear at Appendix 3.

(ii) The reporting accountant does not carry out a detailed check for compliance, but has a duty to report on any substantial departures from the guidelines discovered whilst carrying out work in preparation of his or her report (see rules 43 and 44(e)).

Rule 30 – Restrictions on transfers between clients

(1) A paper transfer of money held in a *general client account* from the ledger of one *client* to the ledger of another *client* may only be made if:

    (a) it would have been permissible to withdraw that sum from the account under rule 22(1); and

    (b) it would have been permissible to pay that sum into the account under rule 15;

(but there is no requirement in the case of a paper transfer for the written authority of a solicitor, etc., under rule 23(1)).

(2) No sum in respect of a private loan from one *client* to another can be paid out of funds held for the lender either:

    (a) by a payment from one *client account* to another;

    (b) by a paper transfer from the ledger of the lender to that of the borrower; or

    (c) to the borrower directly,

except with the prior written authority of both *clients*.

Notes

(i) "Private loan" means a loan other than one provided by an institution which provides loans on standard terms in the normal course of its activities – rule 30(2) does not apply to loans made by an institutional lender. See also practice rule 6, which prohibits a solicitor from acting for both lender and borrower in a private mortgage at arm's length.

(ii) If the loan is to be made by (or to) joint clients, the consent of each client must be obtained.

Rule 31 – Recognised bodies

(1) If a *solicitors'* practice owns all the shares in a *recognised body* which is an executor, trustee or nominee company, the practice and the *recognised body* must not operate shared *client accounts*, but may:

    (a) use one set of accounting records for money held, received or paid by the practice and the *recognised body*; and/or

    (b) deliver a single accountant's report for both the practice and the *recognised body*.

(2) If a *recognised body* as nominee receives a dividend cheque made out to the *recognised body*, and forwards the cheque, either endorsed or subject to equivalent instructions, to the share-owner's *bank* or *building society*, etc., the *recognised body* will have received (and paid) *controlled trust money*. One way of complying with rule 32

(accounting records) is to keep a copy of the letter to the share-owner's *bank* or *building society*, etc., on the file, and, in accordance with rule 32(14), to keep another copy in a central book of such letters. (See also rule 32(9)(f) (retention of records for six years).)

Notes

(i)   Rule 31(1) applies equally to a recognised body owned by a sole practitioner, or by a multi-national partnership, or indeed by another recognised body.

(ii)   If a recognised body holds or receives money as executor, trustee or nominee, it is a controlled trustee.

Rule 32 – Accounting records for client accounts, etc.

Accounting records which must be kept

(1)   A *solicitor* must at all times keep accounting records properly written up to show the *solicitor's* dealings with:

 (a)   *client money* received, held or paid by the *solicitor*; including *client money* held outside a *client account* under rule 16(1)(a);

 (b)   *controlled trust money* received, held or paid by the *solicitor*; including *controlled trust money* held under rule 18(c) in accordance with the *trustee's* powers in an account which is not a *client account*; and

 (c)   any *office money* relating to any *client* matter, or to any *controlled trust* matter.

(2)   All dealings with *client money* (whether for a *client* or other person), and with any *controlled trust money*, must be appropriately recorded:

 (a)   in a client cash account or in a record of sums transferred from one client ledger account to another; and

 (b)   on the client side of a separate client ledger account for each *client* (or other person, or *controlled trust*).

No other entries may be made in these records.

(3)   If s*eparate designated client accounts* are used:

 (a)   a combined cash account must be kept in order to show the total amount held in *separate designated client accounts*; and

 (b)   a record of the amount held for each *client* (or other person, or *controlled trust*) must be made either in a deposit column of a client ledger account, or on the client side of a client ledger account kept specifically for a *separate designated client account*, for each *client* (or other person, or *controlled trust*).

(4)   All dealings with *office money* relating to any *client* matter, or to any *controlled trust* matter, must be appropriately recorded in an office cash account and on the office side of the appropriate client ledger account.

Current balance

(5)   The current balance on each client ledger account must always be shown, or be readily ascertainable, from the records kept in accordance with paragraphs (2) and (3) above.

Acting for both lender and borrower

(6)   When acting for both lender and borrower on a mortgage advance, separate client ledger accounts for both *clients* need not be opened, provided that:

    (a)   the funds belonging to each *client* are clearly identifiable; and

    (b)   the lender is an institutional lender which provides mortgages on standard terms in the normal course of its activities.

Reconciliations

(7)   The *solicitor* must, at least once every fourteen weeks for *controlled trust money* held in passbook-operated *separate designated client accounts*, and at least once every five weeks in all other cases:

    (a)   compare the balance on the client cash account(s) with the balances shown on the statements and passbooks (after allowing for all unpresented items) of all *general client accounts* and *separate designated client accounts*, and of any account which is not a *client account* but in which the *solicitor* holds *client money* under rule 16(1)(a) (or *controlled trust money* under rule 18(c)), and any *client money* (or *controlled trust money*) held by the *solicitor* in cash; and

    (b)   as at the same date prepare a listing of all the balances shown by the client ledger accounts of the liabilities to *clients* (and other persons, and *controlled trusts*) and compare the total of those balances with the balance on the client cash account; and also

    (c)   prepare a reconciliation statement; this statement must show the cause of the difference, if any, shown by each of the above comparisons.

Bills and notifications of costs

(8)   The *solicitor* must keep readily accessible a central record or file of copies of:

    (a)   all bills given or sent by the *solicitor*; and

    (b)   all other written notifications of *costs* given or sent by the *solicitor*;

in both cases distinguishing between *fees*, *disbursements* not yet paid at the date of the bill, and paid *disbursements*.

Retention of records

(9)   The *solicitor* must retain for at least six years from the date of the last entry:

    (a)   all documents or other records required by paragraphs (1) to (8) above;

    (b)   all statements and passbooks, as printed and issued by the *bank*, *building society* or other financial institution, and/or all duplicate statements and copies of passbook entries permitted in lieu of the originals by rule 10(3) or (4), for:

        (i)   any *general client account* or *separate designated client account*;

        (ii)   any joint account held under rule 10;

      (iii)   any account which is not a *client account* but in which the *solicitor* holds *client money* under rule 16(1)(a);

      (iv)   any account which is not a *client account* but in which *controlled trust money* is held under rule 18(c); and

      (v)   any *office account* maintained in relation to the practice;

(c)   any records kept under rule 9 (liquidators, trustees in bankruptcy, Court of Protection receivers and trustees of occupational pension schemes) including, as printed or otherwise issued, any statements, passbooks and other accounting records originating outside the *solicitor's* office;

(d)   any written instructions to withhold *client money* from a *client account* (or a copy of the *solicitor's* confirmation of oral instructions) in accordance with rule 16;

(e)   any central registers kept under paragraphs (11) to (13) below; and

(f)   any copy letters kept centrally under rule 31(2) (dividend cheques endorsed over by recognised body).

(10) The *solicitor* must retain for at least two years:

(a)   originals or copies of all authorities, other than cheques, for the withdrawal of money from a *client account*; and

(b)   all original paid cheques (or digital images of the front and back of all original paid cheques), unless there is a written arrangement with the *bank*, *building society* or other financial institution that:

      (i)   it will retain the original cheques on the *solicitor's* behalf for that period; or

      (ii)   in the event of destruction of any original cheques, it will retain digital images of the front and back of those cheques on the *solicitor's* behalf for that period and will, on demand by the *solicitor*, the *solicitor's* reporting accountant or the *Society*, produce copies of the digital images accompanied, when requested, by a certificate of verification signed by an authorised officer.

Centrally kept records for certain accounts, etc.

(11) Statements and passbooks for *client money* or *controlled trust money* held outside a *client account* under rule 16(1)(a) or rule 18(c) must be kept together centrally, or the *solicitor* must maintain a central register of these accounts.

(12) Any records kept under rule 9 (liquidators, trustees in bankruptcy, Court of Protection receivers and trustees of occupational pension schemes) must be kept together centrally, or the *solicitor* must maintain a central register of the appointments.

(13) The statements, passbooks, duplicate statements and copies of passbook entries relating to any joint account held under rule 10 must be kept together centrally, or the *solicitor* must maintain a central register of all joint accounts.

(14) If a *recognised body* as nominee follows the option in rule 31(2) (keeping instruction letters for dividend payments), a central book must be kept of all instruction letters to the share-owner's *bank* or *building society*, etc.

Computerisation

(15) Records required by this rule may be kept on a computerised system, apart from the following documents, which must be retained as printed or otherwise issued:

(a) original statements and passbooks retained under paragraph (9)(b) above;

(b) original statements, passbooks and other accounting records retained under paragraph (9)(c) above; and

(c) original cheques and copy authorities retained under paragraph (10) above.

There is no obligation to keep a hard copy of computerised records. However, if no hard copy is kept, the information recorded must be capable of being reproduced reasonably quickly in printed form for at least six years.

Suspense ledger accounts

(16) Suspense client ledger accounts may be used only when the *solicitor* can justify their use; for instance, for temporary use on receipt of an unidentified payment, if time is needed to establish the nature of the payment or the identity of the *client*.

Notes

(i)   It is strongly recommended that accounting records are written up at least weekly, even in the smallest practice, and daily in the case of larger firms.

(ii)   Rule 32(1) to (6) (general record-keeping requirements) and rule 32(7) (reconciliations) do not apply to:

(a) solicitor liquidators, trustees in bankruptcy, Court of Protection receivers and trustees of occupational pension schemes operating in accordance with statutory rules or regulations under rule 9(1)(a);

(b) joint accounts operated under rule 10;

(c) a client's own account operated under rule 11; the record-keeping requirements for this type of account are set out in rule 33;

(d) controlled trustees who instruct an outside manager to run, or continue to run, on a day-to-day basis, the business or property portfolio of an estate or trust, provided the manager keeps and retains appropriate accounting records, which are available for inspection by the Society in accordance with rule 34. (See also note (v) to rule 23.)

(iii)   When a cheque or draft is received on behalf of a client and is endorsed over, not passing through a client account, it must be recorded in the books of account as a receipt and payment on behalf of the client. The same applies to cash received and not deposited in a client account but paid out to or on behalf of a client. A cheque made payable to a client, which is forwarded to the client by the solicitor, is not client money and falls outside the rules, although it is advisable to record the action taken.

(iv)   For the purpose of rule 32, money which has been paid into a client account under rule 19(1)(c) (receipt of costs), or under rule 20(2)(b) (mixed money), and for the time being remains in a client account, is to be treated as client money; it should be recorded on the client side of the client ledger account, but must be appropriately identified.

(v)   For the purpose of rule 32, money which has been paid into an office account under rule 19(1)(b) (receipt of costs), rule 21(1)(a) (advance payments from the Legal Services Commission), or under rule 21(1)(b) (payment of costs from the Legal Services Commission), and for the time being remains in an office account without breaching the rules, is to be treated as office money. Money paid into an office account under rule 21(2)(b) (regular payments) is office money. All these payments should be recorded on the office side of the client ledger account (for the individual client or for the Legal Services Commission), and must be appropriately identified.

(vi) Some accounting systems do not retain a record of past daily balances. This does not put the solicitor in breach of rule 32(5).

(vii) "Clearly identifiable" in rule 32(6) means that by looking at the ledger account the nature and owner of the mortgage advance are unambiguously stated. For example, if a mortgage advance of £100,000 is received from the ABC Building Society, the entry should be recorded as "£100,000, mortgage advance, ABC Building Society". It is not enough to state that the money was received from the ABC Building Society without specifying the nature of the payment, or vice versa.

(viii) Although the solicitor does not open a separate ledger account for the lender, the mortgage advance credited to that account belongs to the lender, not to the borrower, until completion takes place. Improper removal of these mortgage funds from a client account would be a breach of rule 22.

(ix) Reconciliations should be carried out as they fall due, and in any event no later than the due date for the next reconciliation. In the case of a separate designated client account operated with a passbook, there is no need to ask the bank, building society or other financial institution for confirmation of the balance held. In the case of other separate designated client accounts, the solicitor should either obtain statements at least monthly, or should obtain written confirmation of the balance direct from the bank, building society or other financial institution. There is no requirement to check that interest has been credited since the last statement, or the last entry in the passbook.

(x) In making the comparisons under rule 32(7)(a) and (b), some solicitors use credits of one client against debits of another when checking total client liabilities. This is improper because it fails to show up the shortage.

(xi) The effect of rule 32(9)(b) is that the solicitor must ensure that the bank issues hard copy statements. Statements sent from the bank to its solicitor customer by means of electronic mail, even if capable of being printed off as hard copies, will not suffice.

(xii) Rule 32(9)(d) – retention of client's instructions to withhold money from a client account – does not require records to be kept centrally; however, this may be prudent, to avoid losing the instructions if the file is passed to the client.

(xiii) A solicitor who holds client money (or controlled trust money) in a currency other than sterling should hold that money in a separate account for the appropriate currency. Separate books of account should be kept for that currency.

(xiv) The requirement to keep paid cheques under rule 32(10)(b) extends to all cheques drawn on a client account, or on an account in which client money is held outside a client account under rule 16(1)(a), or on an account in which controlled trust money is held outside a client account under rule 18(c).

(xv) Solicitors may enter into an arrangement whereby the bank keeps digital images of paid cheques in place of the originals. The bank should take an electronic image of the front and back of each cheque in black and white and agree to hold such images, and to make printed copies available on request, for at least two years. Alternatively, solicitors may take and keep their own digital images of paid cheques.

(xvi) Microfilmed copies of paid cheques are not acceptable for the purposes of rule 32(10)(b). If a bank is able to provide microfilmed copies only, the solicitor must obtain the original paid cheques from the bank and retain them for at least two years.

(xvii) Certificates of verification in relation to digital images of cheques may on occasion be required by the Society when exercising its investigative and enforcement powers. The reporting accountant will not need to ask for a certificate of verification but will be able to rely on the printed copy of the digital image as if it were the original.

Rule 33 – Accounting records for clients' own accounts

(1)   When a *solicitor* operates a *client's* own account as signatory under rule 11, the *solicitor* must retain, for at least six years from the date of the last entry, the statements or passbooks as printed and issued by the *bank*, *building society* or other financial institution, and/or the duplicate statements, copies of passbook entries and cheque details permitted in lieu of the originals by rule 11(3) or (4); and any central register kept under paragraph (2) below.

(2)   The *solicitor* must either keep these records together centrally, or maintain a central register of the accounts operated under rule 11.

(3)   If, when the *solicitor* ceases to operate the account, the *client* requests the original statements or passbooks, the *solicitor* must take photocopies and keep them in lieu of the originals.

(4)   This rule applies only to *solicitors* in private practice.

Note

Solicitors should remember the requirements of rule 32(8) (central record of bills, etc.).

PART E – MONITORING AND INVESTIGATION BY THE SOCIETY

Rule 34 – Production of records

(1)   Any *solicitor* must at the time and place fixed by the *Society* produce to any person appointed by the *Society* any records, papers, *client* and *controlled trust* matter files, financial accounts and other documents, and any other information, necessary to enable preparation of a report on compliance with the rules.

(2)   A requirement for production under paragraph (1) above must be in writing, and left at or sent by registered post or recorded delivery to the most recent address held by the *Society's* Regulation and Information Services department, or delivered by the *Society's* appointee. If sent through the post, receipt will be deemed 48 hours (excluding Saturdays, Sundays and Bank Holidays) after posting.

(3)   Material kept electronically must be produced in the form required by the *Society's* appointee.

(4)   The *Society's* appointee is entitled to seek verification from *clients* and staff, and from the *banks*, *building societies* and other financial institutions used by the *solicitor*. The *solicitor* must, if necessary, provide written permission for the information to be given.

(5)   The *Society's* appointee is not entitled to take original documents away but must be provided with photocopies on request.

(6)   A *solicitor* must be prepared to explain and justify any departures from the guidelines for accounting procedures and systems published by the *Society* (see rule 29).

(7)   Any report made by the *Society's* appointee may, if appropriate, be sent to the Crown Prosecution Service or the Serious Fraud Office and/or used in proceedings before the Solicitors' Disciplinary Tribunal. In the case of a *registered European lawyer* or

registered foreign lawyer, the report may also be sent to the competent authority in that lawyer's home state or states. In the case of a *solicitor of the Supreme Court* who is established in another state under the Establishment of Lawyers Directive 98/5/EC, the report may also be sent to the competent authority in the host state. The report may also be sent to any of the accountancy bodies set out in rule 37(1)(a) and/or taken into account by the *Society* in relation to a possible disqualification of a reporting accountant under rule 37(3).

(8) Without prejudice to paragraph (1) above, any *solicitor* must produce documents relating to any account kept by the *solicitor* at a *bank* or with a *building society*:

    (a)   in connection with the *solicitor's* practice; or

    (b)   in connection with any *trust* of which the *solicitor* is or formerly was a *trustee*,

for inspection by a person appointed by the *Society* for the purpose of preparing a report on compliance with the rules or on whether the account has been used for or in connection with a breach of any other rules, codes or guidance made or issued by the Council of the *Society*. Paragraphs (2)–(7) above apply in relation to this paragraph in the same way as to paragraph (1).

Notes

(i)   "Solicitor" in rule 34 (as elsewhere in the rules) includes any person to whom the rules apply – see rule 2(2)(x), rule 4 and note (ii) to rule 4.

(ii)   The Society's powers override any confidence or privilege between solicitor and client.

(iii)   The Society's monitoring and investigation powers are exercised by Forensic Investigations, Office for the Supervision of Solicitors.

(iv)   Reasons are never given for a visit by Forensic Investigations, so as:

    (a)   to safeguard the Society's sources of information; and

    (b)   not to alert a defaulting principal or employee to conceal or compound his or her misappropriations.

(v)   Rule 34(8) does not apply to registered foreign lawyers in the absence of an order by the Lord Chancellor under section 89(5) of the Courts and Legal Services Act 1990. The Society can nevertheless exercise the powers under rule 34(8) in the case of a multi-national partnership, because the rule applies to those partners who are solicitors or registered European lawyers even though it does not apply to the registered foreign lawyers.

PART F – ACCOUNTANTS' REPORTS

Rule 35 – Delivery of accountants' reports

A *solicitor of the Supreme Court*, *registered European lawyer*, *registered foreign lawyer* or *recognised body* who or which has, at any time during an *accounting period*, held or received *client money* or *controlled trust money*, or operated a *client's* own account as signatory, must deliver to the *Society* an accountant's report for that *accounting period* within six months of the end of the *accounting period*. This duty extends to the directors of such a *recognised body* if it is a company, and to the members of such a *recognised body* if it is a limited liability partnership.

Notes

(i)   Section 34 of the Solicitors Act 1974 requires every solicitor of the Supreme Court to deliver an accountant's report once in every twelve months ending 31st October, unless the Society is satisfied that this is unnecessary. This provision is applied to recognised bodies by the Administration of Justice Act 1985, Schedule 2, paragraph 5(1). The Courts and Legal Services Act 1990, Schedule 14, paragraph 8(1) imposes the same duty on registered foreign lawyers, and this provision is extended to registered European lawyers by the European Communities (Lawyer's Practice) Regulations 2000, Schedule 4, paragraph 5(2). In general, the Society is satisfied that no report is necessary when the rules do not require a report to be delivered, but this is without prejudice to the Society's overriding discretion. In addition, a condition imposed on a solicitor's practising certificate under section 12(4)(b) of the Solicitors Act 1974 may require the solicitor to deliver accountant's reports at more frequent intervals.

(ii)   A solicitor who practises only in one or more of the ways set out in rule 5 is exempt from the rules, and therefore does not have to deliver an accountant's report.

(iii)   The requirement in rule 35 for a registered foreign lawyer to deliver an accountant's report applies only to a registered foreign lawyer practising in partnership with a solicitor of the Supreme Court or registered European lawyer, or as a director of a recognised body which is a company, or as a member of a recognised body which is a limited liability partnership.

(iv)   The form of report is dealt with in rule 47.

(v)   When client money is held or received by a practice, the principals in the practice (including those held out as principals) will have held or received client money. A salaried partner whose name is included in the list of partners on a firm's letterhead, even if the name appears under a separate heading of "salaried partners" or "associate partners", has been held out as a principal.

(va)   In the case of an incorporated practice, it is the company or limited liability partnership (i.e. the recognised body) which will have held or received client money. The recognised body and its directors (in the case of a company) or members (in the case of a limited liability partnership) will have the duty to deliver an accountant's report, although the directors or members will not usually have held client money.

(vi)   Assistant solicitors and consultants do not normally hold client money. An assistant solicitor or consultant might be a signatory for a firm's client account, but this does not constitute holding or receiving client money. If a client or third party hands cash to an assistant solicitor or consultant, it is the sole principal or the partners (rather than the assistant solicitor or consultant) who are regarded as having received and held the money. In the case of a recognised body, whether a company or a limited liability partnership, it would be the recognised body itself which would be regarded as having held or received the money.

(vii)   If, exceptionally, an assistant solicitor or consultant has a client account (for example, as a controlled trustee), or operates a client's own account as signatory, the assistant solicitor or consultant will have to deliver an accountant's report. The assistant solicitor or consultant can be included in the report of the practice, but must ensure that his or her name is added, and an explanation given.

(viii) A solicitor to whom a cheque or draft is made out, and who in the course of practice endorses it over to a client or employer, has received (and paid) client money. That solicitor will have to deliver an accountant's report, even if no other client money has been held or received.

(ix)   When only a small number of transactions is undertaken or a small volume of client money is handled in an accounting period, a waiver of the obligation to deliver a report may sometimes be granted. Applications should be made to Regulation and Information Services.

(x)   If a solicitors' practice owns all the shares in a recognised body which is an executor, trustee or nominee company, the practice and the recognised body may deliver a single accountant's report (see rule 31(1)(b)).

Rule 36 – Accounting periods

The norm

(1)   An "accounting period" means the period for which the accounts of the *solicitor* are ordinarily made up, except that it must:

(a)   begin at the end of the previous *accounting period*; and

(b)   cover twelve months.

Paragraphs (2) to (5) below set out exceptions.

First and resumed reports

(2)   For a *solicitor* who is under a duty to deliver his or her first report, the *accounting period* must begin on the date when the *solicitor* first held or received *client money* or *controlled trust money* (or operated a *client's* own account as signatory), and may cover less than twelve months.

(3)   For a *solicitor* who is under a duty to deliver his or her first report after a break, the *accounting period* must begin on the date when the *solicitor* for the first time after the break held or received *client money* or *controlled trust money* (or operated a *client's* own account as signatory), and may cover less than twelve months.

Change of accounting period

(4)   If a practice changes the period for which its accounts are made up (for example, on a merger, or simply for convenience), the *accounting period* immediately preceding the change may be shorter than twelve months, or longer than twelve months up to a maximum of 18 months, provided that the *accounting period* shall not be changed to a period longer than twelve months unless the Law Society receives written notice of the change before expiry of the deadline for delivery of the accountant's report which would have been expected on the basis of the firm's old *accounting period*.

Final reports

(5)   A *solicitor* who for any reason stops holding or receiving *client money* or *controlled trust money* (and operating any *client's* own account as signatory) must deliver a final report. The *accounting period* must end on the date upon which the *solicitor* stopped holding or receiving *client money* or *controlled trust money* (and operating any *client's* own account as signatory), and may cover less than twelve months.

Notes

(i)   In the case of solicitors joining or leaving a continuing partnership, any accountant's report for the practice as a whole will show the names and dates of the principals joining or leaving. For a solicitor who did not previously hold or receive client money, etc., and has become a principal in the firm, the report for the practice will represent, from the date of joining, the solicitor's first report for the purpose of rule 36(2). For a solicitor who was a principal in the firm and, on leaving, stops holding or receiving client money, etc., the report for the practice will represent, up to the date of leaving, the solicitor's final report for the purpose of rule 36(5) above.

(ii)   When a partnership splits up, it is usually appropriate for the books to be made up as at the date of dissolution, and for an accountant's report to be delivered within six months of that date. If, however, the old partnership continues to hold or receive client money, etc., in connection with outstanding matters, accountant's reports will continue to be required for those matters; the books should then be made up on completion of the last of those matters and a report delivered within six months of that date. The same would be true for a sole practitioner winding up matters on retirement.

(iii)   When a practice is being wound up, the solicitor may be left with money which is unattributable, or belongs to a client who cannot be traced. It may be appropriate to apply to the Society for authority to withdraw this money from the solicitor's client account – see rule 22(1)(h), rule 22(2)(h), and note (viii) to rule 22.

Rule 37 – Qualifications for making a report

(1)   A report must be prepared and signed by an accountant

    (a)   who is a member of:

        (i)   the Institute of Chartered Accountants in England and Wales;

        (ii)   the Institute of Chartered Accountants of Scotland;

        (iii)   the Association of Chartered Certified Accountants;

        (iv)   the Institute of Chartered Accountants in Ireland; or

        (v)   the Association of Authorised Public Accountants; **and**

    (b)   who is also:

        (i)   an individual who is a registered auditor within the terms of section 35(1)(a) of the Companies Act 1989; or

        (ii)   an employee of such an individual; or

        (iii)   a *partner* in or employee of a *partnership* which is a registered auditor within the terms of section 35(1)(a) of the Companies Act 1989; or

        (iv)   a director or employee of a company which is a registered auditor within the terms of section 35(1)(a) of the Companies Act 1989; or

        (v)   a member or employee of a limited liability partnership which is a registered auditor within the terms of section 35(1)(a) of the Companies Act 1989.

(2)   An accountant is not qualified to make a report if:

    (a)   at any time between the beginning of the *accounting period* to which the report relates, and the completion of the report:

        (i)   he or she was a *partner* or employee, or an officer or employee (in the case of a company), or a member or employee (in the case of a limited liability partnership) in the practice to which the report relates; or

        (ii)   he or she was employed by the same *non-solicitor employer* as the *solicitor* for whom the report is being made; or

    (b)   he or she has been disqualified under paragraph (3) below and notice of disqualification has been given under paragraph (4) (and has not subsequently been withdrawn).

(3)   The *Society* may disqualify an accountant from making any accountant's report if:

(a)   the accountant has been found guilty by his or her professional body of professional misconduct or discreditable conduct; or

(b)   the *Society* is satisfied that a *solicitor* has not complied with the rules in respect of matters which the accountant has negligently failed to specify in a report.

In coming to a decision, the *Society* will take into account any representations made by the accountant or his or her professional body.

(4)   Written notice of disqualification must be left at or sent by registered post or recorded delivery to the address of the accountant shown on an accountant's report or in the records of the accountant's professional body. If sent through the post, receipt will be deemed 48 hours (excluding Saturdays, Sundays and Bank Holidays) after posting.

(5)   An accountant's disqualification may be notified to any *solicitor* likely to be affected and may be printed in the Law Society's Gazette or other publication.

Note

It is not a breach of the rules for a solicitor to retain an outside accountant to write up the books of account and to instruct the same accountant to prepare the accountant's report. However, the accountant will have to disclose these circumstances in the report – see the form of report in Appendix 5.

Rule 38 – Reporting accountant's rights and duties – letter of engagement

(1)   The *solicitor* must ensure that the reporting accountant's rights and duties are stated in a letter of engagement incorporating the following terms:

"In accordance with rule 38 of the Solicitors' Accounts Rules 1998, you are instructed as follows:

(i)   that you may, and are encouraged to, report directly to the Law Society without prior reference to me/this firm/this company/this limited liability partnership should you, during the course of carrying out work in preparation of the accountant's report, discover evidence of theft or fraud affecting client money, controlled trust money, or money in a client's own account operated by a solicitor (or registered European lawyer, or registered foreign lawyer, or recognised body) as signatory; or information which is likely to be of material significance in determining whether any solicitor (or registered European lawyer, or registered foreign lawyer, or recognised body) is a fit and proper person to hold client money or controlled trust money, or to operate a client's own account as signatory;

(ii)   to report directly to the Law Society should your appointment be terminated following the issue of, or indication of intention to issue, a qualified accountant's report, or following the raising of concerns prior to the preparation of an accountant's report;

(iii) to deliver to me/this firm/this company/this limited liability partnership with your report the completed checklist required by rule 46 of the Solicitors' Accounts Rules 1998; to retain for at least three years from the date of signature a copy of the completed checklist; and to produce the copy to the Law Society on request;

(iv) to retain these terms of engagement for at least three years after the termination of the retainer and to produce them to the Law Society on request; and

(v) following any direct report made to the Law Society under (i) or (ii) above, to provide to the Law Society on request any further relevant information in your possession or in the possession of your firm.

To the extent necessary to enable you to comply with (i) to (v) above, I/we waive my/the firm's/the company's/the limited liability partnership's right of confidentiality. This waiver extends to any report made, document produced or information disclosed to the Law Society in good faith pursuant to these instructions, even though it may subsequently transpire that you were mistaken in your belief that there was cause for concern."

(2) The letter of engagement and a copy must be signed by the *solicitor* (or by a *partner*, or in the case of a company by a director, or in the case of a limited liability partnership by a member) and by the accountant. The *solicitor* must keep the copy of the signed letter of engagement for at least three years after the termination of the retainer and produce it to the *Society* on request.

Notes

(i) Any direct report by the accountant to the Society under rule 38(1)(i) or (ii) should be made to the Office for the Supervision of Solicitors.

(ii) Rule 38(1) envisages that the specified terms are incorporated in a letter from the solicitor to the accountant. Instead, the specified terms may be included in a letter from the accountant to the solicitor setting out the terms of the engagement. If so, the text must be adapted appropriately. The letter must be signed in duplicate by both parties – the solicitor will keep the original, and the accountant the copy.

Rule 39 – Change of accountant

On instructing an accountancy practice to replace that previously instructed to produce accountant's reports, the *solicitor* must immediately notify the *Society* of the change and provide the name and business address of the new accountancy practice.

Rule 40 – Place of examination

Unless there are exceptional circumstances, the place of examination of a *solicitor's* accounting records, files and other relevant documents must be the *solicitor's* office and not the office of the accountant. This does not prevent an initial electronic transmission of data to the accountant for examination at the accountant's office with a view to reducing the time which needs to be spent at the solicitor's office.

Rule 41 – Provision of details of bank accounts, etc.

The accountant must request, and the *solicitor* must provide, details of all accounts kept or operated by the *solicitor* in connection with the *solicitor's* practice at any *bank*, *building society* or other financial institution at any time during the *accounting period* to which the report relates. This includes *client accounts, office accounts,* accounts which are not *client accounts* but which contain *client money* or *controlled trust money*, and *clients'* own accounts operated by the *solicitor* as signatory.

Rule 42 – Test procedures

(1)   The accountant must examine the accounting records (including statements and passbooks), *client* and *controlled trust* matter files selected by the accountant as and when appropriate, and other relevant documents of the *solicitor*, and make the following checks and tests:

   (a)   confirm that the accounting system in every office of the *solicitor* complies with:

   ▶   rule 32 – accounting records for client accounts, etc.;

   ▶   rule 33 – accounting records for clients' own accounts;

   and is so designed that:

   (i)   an appropriate client ledger account is kept for each *client* (or other person for whom *client money* is received, held or paid) and each *controlled trust*;

   (ii)   the client ledger accounts show separately from other information details of all *client money* and *controlled trust money* received, held or paid on account of each *client* (or other person for whom *client money* is received, held or paid) and each *controlled trust*; and

   (iii)   transactions relating to *client money*, *controlled trust money* and any other money dealt with through a *client account* are recorded in the accounting records in a way which distinguishes them from transactions relating to any other money received, held or paid by the *solicitor*;

   (b)   make test checks of postings to the client ledger accounts from records of receipts and payments of *client money* and *controlled trust money*, and make test checks of the casts of these accounts and records;

   (c)   compare a sample of payments into and from the *client accounts* as shown in *bank* and *building society* statements or passbooks with the *solicitor's* records of receipts and payments of *client money* and *controlled trust money*;

   (d)   test check the system of recording *costs* and of making transfers in respect of *costs* from the *client accounts*;

   (e)   make a test examination of a selection of documents requested from the *solicitor* in order to confirm:

   (i)   that the financial transactions (including those giving rise to transfers from one client ledger account to another) evidenced by such documents comply with Parts A and B of the rules, rule 30 (restrictions on transfers between clients) and rule 31 (recognised bodies); and

   (ii)   that the entries in the accounting records reflect those transactions in a manner complying with rule 32;

   (f)   subject to paragraph (2) below, extract (or check extractions of) balances on the client ledger accounts during the *accounting period* under review at not fewer than two dates selected by the accountant (one of which may be the last day of the *accounting period*), and at each date:

   (i)   compare the total shown by the client ledger accounts of the liabilities to the *clients* (or other persons for whom *client money* is held) and *controlled trusts* with the cash account balance; and

(ii)   reconcile that cash account balance with the balances held in the *client accounts*, and accounts which are not *client accounts* but in which *client money* or *controlled trust money* is held, as confirmed direct to the accountant by the relevant *banks*, *building societies* and other financial institutions;

(g)   confirm that reconciliation statements have been made and kept in accordance with rule 32(7) and (9)(a);

(h)   make a test examination of the client ledger accounts to see whether payments from the *client account* have been made on any individual account in excess of money held on behalf of that *client* (or other person for whom *client money* is held) or *controlled trust*;

(i)   check the office ledgers, office cash accounts and the statements provided by the *bank*, *building society* or other financial institution for any *office account* maintained by the *solicitor* in connection with the practice, to see whether any *client money* or *controlled trust money* has been improperly paid into an *office account* or, if properly paid into an *office account* under rule 19(1)(b) or rule 21(1), has been kept there in breach of the rules;

(j)   check the accounting records kept under rule 32(9)(d) and (11) for *client money* held outside a *client account* to ascertain what transactions have been effected in respect of this money and to confirm that the *client* has given appropriate instructions under rule 16(1)(a);

(k)   make a test examination of the client ledger accounts to see whether rule 32(6) (accounting records when acting for both lender and borrower) has been complied with;

(l)   for liquidators, trustees in bankruptcy, Court of Protection receivers and trustees of occupational pension schemes, check that records are being kept in accordance with rule 32(8), (9)(c) and (12), and cross-check transactions with *client* or *controlled trust* matter files when appropriate;

(m)   check that statements and passbooks and/or duplicate statements and copies of passbook entries are being kept in accordance with rule 32(9)(b)(ii) and (13) (record-keeping requirements for joint accounts), and cross-check transactions with *client* matter files when appropriate;

(n)   check that statements and passbooks and/or duplicate statements, copies of passbook entries and cheque details are being kept in accordance with rule 33 (record-keeping requirements for clients' own accounts), and cross-check transactions with *client* matter files when appropriate;

(o)   check that interest earned on *separate designated client accounts*, and in accounts opened on *clients'* instructions under rule 16(1)(a), is credited in accordance with rule 24(1) and (6)(a), and note (i) to rule 24;

(p)   in the case of private practice only, check that for the period which will be covered by the accountant's report (excluding any part of that period falling before 1st September 2000) the practice was covered for the purposes of the Solicitors' Indemnity Insurance Rules 2000 in respect of its offices in England and Wales by:

▶   certificates of qualifying insurance outside the assigned risks pool; or

▶ a policy issued by the assigned risks pool manager; or

▶ certificates of indemnity cover under the professional requirements of a *registered European lawyer's* home jurisdiction in accordance with paragraph 1 of Appendix 4 to those Rules; or

▶ certificates of additional insurance with a qualifying insurer under paragraph 2 of Appendix 4 to those Rules; and

(q) ask for any information and explanations required as a result of making the above checks and tests.

Extracting balances

(2) For the purposes of paragraph (1)(f) above, if a *solicitor* uses a computerised or mechanised system of accounting which automatically produces an extraction of all client ledger balances, the accountant need not check all client ledger balances extracted on the list produced by the computer or machine against the individual records of client ledger accounts, provided the accountant:

(a) confirms that a satisfactory system of control is in operation and the accounting records are in balance;

(b) carries out a test check of the extraction against the individual records; and

(c) states in the report that he or she has relied on this exception.

Notes

(i) The rules do not require a complete audit of the solicitor's accounts nor do they require the preparation of a profit and loss account or balance sheet.

(ii) In making the comparisons under rule 42(1)(f), some accountants improperly use credits of one client against debits of another when checking total client liabilities, thus failing to disclose a shortage. A debit balance on a client account when no funds are held for that client results in a shortage which must be disclosed as a result of the comparison.

(iii) The main purpose of confirming balances direct with banks, etc., under rule 42(1)(f)(ii) is to ensure that the solicitor's records accurately reflect the sums held at the bank. The accountant is not expected to conduct an active search for undisclosed accounts.

Rule 43 – Departures from guidelines for accounting procedures and systems

The accountant should be aware of the Council's guidelines for accounting procedures and systems (see rule 29), and must note in the accountant's report any substantial departures from the guidelines discovered whilst carrying out work in preparation of the report. (See also rule 44(e).)

Rule 44 – Matters outside the accountant's remit

The accountant is not required:

(a) to extend his or her enquiries beyond the information contained in the documents produced, supplemented by any information and explanations given by the *solicitor*;

(b)   to enquire into the stocks, shares, other securities or documents of title held by the *solicitor* on behalf of the *solicitor's clients*;

(c)   to consider whether the accounting records of the *solicitor* have been properly written up at any time other than the time at which his or her examination of the accounting records takes place;

(d)   to check compliance with the provisions in rule 24(2) to (5) and (6)(b) on payment of sums in lieu of interest; or

(e)   to make a detailed check on compliance with the guidelines for accounting procedures and systems (see rules 29 and 43).

Rule 45 – Privileged documents

A *solicitor*, acting on a *client's* instructions, always has the right on the grounds of privilege as between *solicitor* and *client* to decline to produce any document requested by the accountant for the purposes of his or her examination. In these circumstances, the accountant must qualify the report and set out the circumstances.

Rule 46 – Completion of checklist

The accountant should exercise his or her professional judgment in adopting a suitable "audit" programme, but must also complete and sign a checklist in the form published from time to time by the Council of the Law Society. The *solicitor* must obtain the completed checklist, retain it for at least three years from the date of signature and produce it to the *Society* on request.

Notes

(i)   The current checklist appears at Appendix 4. It is issued by the Society to solicitors at the appropriate time for completion by their reporting accountants.

(ii)   The letter of engagement required by rule 38 imposes a duty on the accountant to hand the completed checklist to the solicitor, to keep a copy for three years and to produce the copy to the Society on request.

Rule 47 – Form of accountant's report

The accountant must complete and sign his or her report in the form published from time to time by the Council of the Law Society.

Notes

(i)   The current form of accountant's report appears at Appendix 5.

(ii)   The form of report is prepared and issued by the Society to solicitors at the appropriate time for completion by their reporting accountants. Separate reports can be delivered for each principal in a partnership but most firms deliver one report in the name of all the principals. For assistant solicitors and consultants, see rule 35, notes (vi) and (vii).

(iia)   A recognised body will deliver only one report, on behalf of the company and its directors, or on behalf of the limited liability partnership and its members – see rule 35(1).

(iii)   Although it may be agreed that the accountant send the report direct to the Society, the responsibility for delivery is that of the solicitor. The form of report requires the accountant to confirm that either a copy of the report has been sent to each of the solicitors of the Supreme Court, registered European lawyers and registered foreign lawyers to whom the report relates, or a copy of the report has been sent to a named partner on behalf of all the partners in the firm. A similar confirmation is required in respect of the directors of a recognised body which is a company, or the members of a recognised body which is a limited liability partnership.

(iv)   A reporting accountant is not required to report on trivial breaches due to clerical errors or mistakes in book-keeping, provided that they have been rectified on discovery and the accountant is satisfied that no client suffered any loss as a result.

(v)   In many practices, clerical and book-keeping errors will arise. In the majority of cases these may be classified by the reporting accountant as trivial breaches. However, a "trivial breach" cannot be precisely defined. The amount involved, the nature of the breach, whether the breach is deliberate or accidental, how often the same breach has occurred, and the time outstanding before correction (especially the replacement of any shortage) are all factors which should be considered by the accountant before deciding whether a breach is trivial.

(vi)   The Society receives a number of reports which are qualified only by reference to trivial breaches, but which show a significant difference between liabilities to clients and client money held in client and other accounts. An explanation for this difference, from either the accountant or the solicitor, must be given.

(vii)   Accountants' reports should be sent to Regulation and Information Services.

(viii)   For direct reporting by the accountant to the Society in cases of concern, see rule 38 and note (i) to that rule.

Rule 48 – Practices with two or more places of business

If a practice has two or more offices:

(a)   separate reports may be delivered in respect of the different offices; and

(b)   separate *accounting periods* may be adopted for different offices, provided that:

    (i)   separate reports are delivered;

    (ii)   every office is covered by a report delivered within six months of the end of its *accounting period*; and

    (iii)   there are no gaps between the *accounting periods* covered by successive reports for any particular office or offices.

Rule 49 – Waivers

The *Society* may waive in writing in any particular case or cases any of the provisions of Part F of the rules, and may revoke any waiver.

Note

Applications for waivers should be made to Regulation and Information Services. In appropriate cases, solicitors may be granted a waiver of the obligation to deliver an accountant's report (see rule 35, and note (ix) to that rule). The circumstances in which a waiver of any other provision of Part F would be given must be extremely rare.

PART G – COMMENCEMENT

Rule 50 – Commencement

(1) These rules must be implemented not later than 1st May 2000; until a practice implements these rules, it must continue to operate the Solicitors' Accounts Rules 1991.

(2) Practices opting to implement these rules before 1st May 2000 must implement them in their entirety, and not selectively.

(3) Part F of the rules (accountants' reports) will apply to:

(a) reports covering any period of time after 30th April 2000; and also

(b) reports covering any earlier period of time for which a practice has opted to operate these rules.

(4) The Accountant's Report Rules 1991 will continue to apply to:

(a) reports covering any period of time before 22nd July 1998; and also

(b) reports covering any period of time after 21st July 1998 and before 1st May 2000 during which a practice continued to operate the Solicitors' Accounts Rules 1991.

(5) If a practice operated the Solicitors' Accounts Rules 1991 for part of an *accounting period*, and these rules for the rest of the *accounting period*, the practice may, in respect of that *accounting period* ("the transitional accounting period") either:

(a) deliver a single accountant's report covering the whole of the transitional accounting period, made partly under the Accountant's Report Rules 1991 and partly under Part F of these rules, as appropriate; or

(b) deliver a separate accountant's report for each part of the transitional accounting period, one under the Accountant's Report Rules 1991 and the other under Part F of these rules; or

(c) deliver a report under the Accountant's Report Rules 1991 to cover that part of the transitional accounting period during which the practice operated the Solicitors' Accounts Rules 1991; and subsequently a report under Part F of these rules to cover the remaining part of the transitional accounting period plus the whole of the next *accounting period*; or

(d) deliver a report under the Accountant's Report Rules 1991 to cover the last complete *accounting period* during which the practice operated the Solicitors' Accounts Rules 1991 plus that part of the transitional accounting period during which the practice continued to operate those rules; and subsequently a report under Part F of these rules to cover the remaining part of the transitional accounting period.

APPENDIX 1

EFFECT OF SOLICITORS' ACCOUNTS RULES 1998

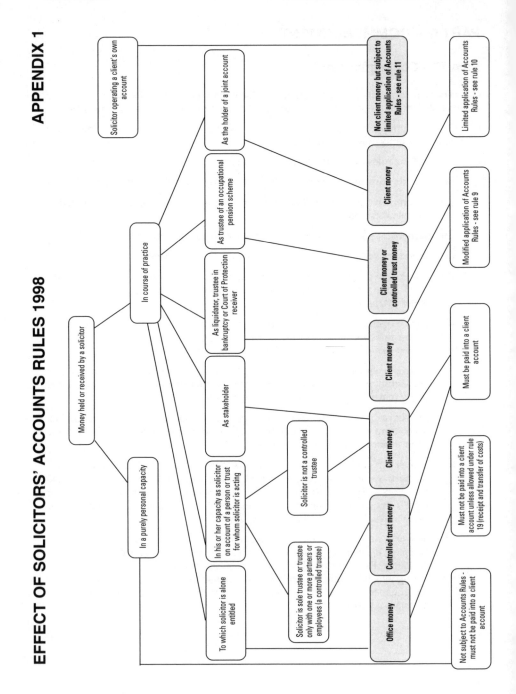

APPENDIX 2

SPECIAL SITUATIONS – WHAT APPLIES

	Is it client money?	Subject to reconciliations?	Keep books?	Retain statements?	Subject to Accountant's Report?	Produce records to Law Society?	Deposit interest?	Retain records generally?	Central records?	Subject to reporting accountant's comparisons?
1 Controlled trust money in client a/c – r.15(1)	No	Yes – r.32(7)	Yes – r.32(1) and (2)	Yes – r.32(9)	Yes – r.42 – same as for client money	Yes – r.34	All interest goes to trust	Yes – r.32(9)	Bills – r.32(8)	Yes – r.42(1)(f) – same as for client money
2 Controlled trust money held outside a client account – r.18	No	Yes – r.32(7)	Yes – r.32(1) and (2)	Yes – r.32(9)	Yes – r.42 – same as for client money	Yes – r.34	All interest goes to trust	Yes – r.32(9)	Bills – r.32(8)	Yes – r.42(1)(f) – same as for client money
3 R.16(1)(a) a/cs in solicitor's name (not client a/c)	Yes	Yes	Yes – r.32(1)(a) and 32(2)	Yes – r.32(9)	Yes	Yes	Yes – r.24	Yes – r.32(9)	Statements or register – r.32(11), bills – r.32(8)	Yes – r.42(1)(f)
4 R.16(1)(b) a/cs in name of client – not operated by solicitor	No	No	No – record solicitor's receipt and payment only	No	No	No	No – all interest earned for client – r.24, note (iii)	No – except record of solicitor's receipt and payment	Bills – r.32(8)	No
5 R.16(1)(b) a/cs in name of client – operated by solicitor	No	No	No – record solicitor's receipt and payment only	Yes – r.33	Limited – r.42(1)(n)	Yes – r.11	No – all interest earned for client – r.24, note (iii)	No – except record of solicitor's receipt and payment	Statements – r.33, Bills – r.32(8)	No
6 Liquidators, trustees in bankruptcy and Court of Protection receivers	Yes – r.9	No – r.9	Modified – statutory records – r.9	Yes – r.9 and r.32(9)(c)	Limited – r.42(1)(l)	Yes – r.9	No – r.9 – comply with statutory rules	Yes – modified r.32(9)(c)	Yes – r.32(12) Bills – r.32(8)	No – r.9
7 Trustees of occupational pension schemes	Will be either client money or controlled trust money	No – r.9	Modified – statutory records – r.9	Yes – r.9 and r.32(9)(c)	Limited – r.42(1)(l)	Yes – r.9	No – r.9 – comply with statutory rules	Yes – modified r.32(9)(c)	Yes – r.32(12) Bills – r.32(8)	No – r.9
8 Joint accounts – r.10	Yes – r.10	No – r.10	No – r.10	Yes – r.10 and r.32(9)(b)(ii)	Limited – r.42(1)(m)	Yes – r.10	No. For joint a/c with client, all interest to client (r.24, note (ix)); for joint a/c with sol. depends on agreement	No – r.10	Statements – r.32(13) Bills – r.32(8)	No – r.10
9 Solicitor acting under power of attorney	Yes	Yes	Yes	Yes	Yes	Yes	Yes	Yes	Bills – r.32(8)	Yes
10 Solicitor operates client's own a/c e.g. under power of attorney – r.11	No	No	No	Yes – r.33	Limited – r.42(1)(n)	Yes – r.11	No – all interest earned for client (r.24, note (iii))	No – r.11	Statements – r.33, Bills – r.32(8)	No
11 Exempt solicitors under r.5	No	No	No	No	No	No	No	No	No	No

APPENDIX 3

LAW SOCIETY GUIDELINES
ACCOUNTING PROCEDURES AND SYSTEMS

1. Introduction

1.1 These guidelines, published under rule 29 of the Solicitors' Accounts Rules 1998, are intended to be a benchmark or broad statement of good practice requirements which should be present in an effective regime for the proper control of client money and controlled trust money. They should therefore be of positive assistance to firms in establishing or reviewing appropriate procedures and systems. They do not override, or detract from the need to comply fully with, the Accounts Rules.

1.2 It should be noted that these guidelines apply equally to client money and to controlled trust money.

1.3 References to partners or firms in the guidelines are intended to include sole practitioners, recognised bodies and their directors (in the case of a company) or members (in the case of a limited liability partnership).

2. General

2.1 Compliance with the Accounts Rules is the equal responsibility of all partners in a firm. They should establish policies and systems to ensure that the firm complies fully with the rules. Responsibility for day-to-day supervision may be delegated to one or more partners to enable effective control to be exercised. Delegation of total responsibility to a cashier or book-keeper is not acceptable.

2.2 The firm should hold a copy of the current version of the Solicitors' Accounts Rules. The person who maintains the books of account must have a full knowledge of the requirements of the rules and the accounting requirements of solicitors' firms.

2.3 Proper books of account should be maintained on the double-entry principle. They should be legible, up to date and contain narratives with the entries which identify and/or provide adequate information about the transaction. Entries should be made in chronological order and the current balance should be shown on client ledger accounts, or be readily ascertainable, in accordance with rule 32(5).

2.4 Ledger accounts for clients, other persons or controlled trusts should include the name of the client or other person or controlled trust and contain a heading which provides a description of the matter or transaction.

2.5 Separate designated client accounts should be brought within the ambit of the systems and procedures for the control of client money and controlled trust money – including reconciliations (see 5.4 below).

2.6 Manual systems for recording client money and controlled trust money are capable of complying with these guidelines and there is no requirement on firms to adopt computerised systems. A computer system, with suitable support procedures will, however, usually provide an efficient means of producing the accounts and associated control information.

2.7 If a computer system is introduced care must be taken to ensure:

(1) that balances transferred from the old books of account are reconciled with the opening balances held on the new system before day-to-day operation commences;

(2) that the new system operates correctly before the old system is abandoned. This may require a period of parallel running of the old and new systems and the satisfactory reconciliation of the two sets of records before the old system ceases.

2.8 The firm should ensure that office account entries in relation to each client or controlled trust matter are maintained up to date as well as the client account entries. Credit balances on office account in respect of client or controlled trust matters should be fully investigated.

2.9 The firm should operate a system to identify promptly situations which may require the payment of deposit interest to clients.

3. Receipt of client money and controlled trust money

3.1 The firm should have procedures for identifying client money and controlled trust money, including cash, when received in the firm, and for promptly recording the receipt of the money either in the books of account or a register for later posting to the client cash book and ledger accounts. The procedures should cover money received through the post, electronically or direct by fee earners or other personnel. They should also cover the safekeeping of money prior to payment to bank.

3.2 The firm should have a system which ensures that client money and controlled trust money is paid promptly into a client account.

3.3 The firm should have a system for identifying money which should not be in a client account and for transferring it without delay.

3.4 The firm should determine a policy and operate a system for dealing with money which is a mixture of office money and client money (or controlled trust money), in compliance with rules 19–21.

4. Payments from client account

4.1 The firm should have clear procedures for ensuring that all withdrawals from client accounts are properly authorised. In particular, suitable persons, consistent with rule 23(1), should be named for the following purposes:

(1) authorisation of internal payment vouchers;

(2) signing client account cheques;

(3) authorising telegraphic or electronic transfers.

No other personnel should be allowed to authorise or sign the documents.

4.2 Persons nominated for the purpose of authorising internal payment vouchers should, for each payment, ensure there is supporting evidence showing clearly the reason for the payment, and the date of it. Similarly, persons signing cheques and authorising transfers should ensure there is a suitable voucher or other supporting evidence to support the payment.

4.3 The firm should have a system for checking the balances on client ledger accounts to ensure no debit balances occur. Where payments are to be made other than out of cleared funds, clear policies and procedures must be in place to ensure that adequate risk assessment is applied.

N.B. If incoming payments are ultimately dishonoured, a debit balance will arise, in breach of the rules, and full replacement of the shortfall will be required under rule 7. See also rule 22, notes (v) and (vi).

4.4 The firm should establish systems for the transfer of costs from client account to office account in accordance with rule 19(2) and (3). Normally transfers should be made only on the basis of rendering a bill or written notification. The payment from the client account should be by way of a cheque or transfer in favour of the firm or sole principal – see rule 23(3)).

4.5 The firm should establish policies and operate systems to control and record accurately any transfers between clients of the firm. Where these arise as a result of loans between clients, the written authority of both the lender and borrower must be obtained in accordance with rule 30(2).

5.   Overall control of client accounts

5.1 The firm should maintain control of all its bank and building society accounts opened for the purpose of holding client money and controlled trust money. In the case of a joint account, a suitable degree of control should be exercised.

5.2 Central records or central registers must be kept in respect of:

(1) accounts held for client money, or controlled trust money, which are not client accounts (rules 16(1)(a), 18(c) and 32(11));

(2) practice as a liquidator, trustee in bankruptcy, Court of Protection receiver or trustee of an occupational pension scheme (rules 9 and 32(12));

(3) joint accounts (rules 10 and 32(13));

(4) dividend payments received by a recognised body as nominee (rules 31(2) and 32(14)); and

(5) clients' own accounts (rules 11, 16(1)(b) and 33(2)).

5.3 In addition, there should be a master list of all:

▶ general client accounts;

▶ separate designated client accounts;

▶ accounts held in respect of 5.2 above; and

▶ office accounts.

The master list should show the current status of each account; e.g. currently in operation or closed with date of closure.

5.4 The firm should operate a system to ensure that accurate reconciliations of the client accounts, whether comprising client and/or controlled trust money, are carried out at least every five weeks or, in the case of passbook-operated separate designated client accounts for controlled trust money, every 14 weeks. In particular it should ensure that:

(1) a full list of client ledger balances is produced. Any debit balances should be listed, fully investigated and rectified immediately. The total of any debit balances cannot be "netted off" against the total of credit balances;

(2) a full list of unpresented cheques is produced;

(3) a list of outstanding lodgments is produced;

(4) formal statements are produced reconciling the client account cash book balances, aggregate client ledger balances and the client bank accounts. All unresolved differences must be investigated and, where appropriate, corrective action taken;

(5) a partner checks the reconciliation statement and any corrective action, and ensures that enquiries are made into any unusual or apparently unsatisfactory items or still unresolved matters.

5.5 Where a computerised system is used, the firm should have clear policies, systems and procedures to control access to client accounts by determining the personnel who should have "write to" and "read only" access. Passwords should be held confidentially by designated personnel and changed regularly to maintain security. Access to the system should not unreasonably be restricted to a single person nor should more people than necessary be given access.

5.6 The firm should establish policies and systems for the retention of the accounting records to ensure:

► books of account, reconciliations, bills, bank statements and passbooks are kept for at least six years;

► paid cheques and other authorities for the withdrawal of money from a client account are kept for at least two years;

► other vouchers and internal expenditure authorisation documents relating directly to entries in the client account books are kept for at least two years.

5.7 The firm should ensure that unused client account cheques are stored securely to prevent unauthorised access. Blank cheques should not be pre-signed. Any cancelled cheques should be retained.

APPENDIX 4   **REPORTING ACCOUNTANT'S CHECKLIST**

SOLICITORS' ACCOUNTS RULES 1998   REPORTING ACCOUNTANT'S CHECKLIST

The following items have been tested to satisfy the examination requirements under
rules 41 - 43, with the results as indicated. Where the position has been found to be
unsatisfactory as a result of these tests, further details have been reported in
section 6 of this checklist or reported by separate appendix.

The Law Society

Name of practice	

Results of test checks:

1. For all client money and controlled trust money	Were any breaches discovered? (Tick the appropriate column.)		If 'yes' should breaches be noted in the accountant's report?		Cross references to audit file documentation
	Yes	No	Yes	No	
(a) Book-keeping system for every office:	Yes	No	Yes	No	
(i) The accounting records satisfactorily distinguish client money and controlled trust money from all other money dealt with by the firm.					
(ii) A separate ledger account is maintained for each client and controlled trust (excepting section (l) below) and the particulars of all client money and controlled trust money received, held or paid on account of each client and controlled trust, including funds held on separate designated deposits, or elsewhere, are recorded.					
(iii) The client ledgers for clients and controlled trusts show a current balance at all times, or the current balance is readily ascertainable.					
(iv) A record of all bills of costs and written notifications has been maintained, which distinguishes profit costs from disbursements, either in the form of a central record or a file of copies of such bills.					
(b) Postings to ledger accounts and casts:	Yes	No	Yes	No	
(i) Postings to ledger accounts for clients and controlled trusts from records of receipts and payments are correct.					
(ii) Casts of ledger accounts for clients and controlled trusts and receipts and payments records are correct.					
(iii) Postings have been recorded in chronological sequence with the date being that of the initiation of the transaction.					
(c) Receipts and payments of client money and controlled trust money:	Yes	No	Yes	No	
(i) Sample receipts and payments of client money and controlled trust money as shown in bank and building society statements have been compared with the firm's records of receipts and payments of client money and controlled trust money, and are correct.					
(ii) Sample paid cheques, or digital images of the front and back of sample paid cheques, have been obtained and details agreed to receipts and payment records.					
(d) System of recording costs and making transfers:	Yes	No	Yes	No	
(i) The firm's system of recording costs has been ascertained and is suitable.					
(ii) Costs have been drawn only where required for or towards payment of the firm's costs where there has been sent to the client a bill of costs or other written notification of the amount of the costs.					
(e) Examination of documents for verification of transactions and entries in accounting records:	Yes	No	Yes	No	
(i) Make a test examination of a number of client and controlled trust files.					

DTP Nov 2001

Results of test checks:

1.　For all client money and controlled trust money	Were any breaches discovered? (Tick the appropriate column.)		If 'yes' should breaches be noted in the accountant's report?		Cross references to audit file documentation
(e) Examination of documents for verification of transactions and entries in accounting records:	Yes	No	Yes	No	
(ii)　All client and controlled trust files requested for examination were made available.					
(iii)　The financial transactions as detailed on client and controlled trust files and other documentation (including transfers from one ledger account to another) were valid and appropriately authorised in accordance with Parts A and B of the Solicitors' Accounts Rules 1998 (SAR).					
(iv)　The financial transactions evidenced by documents on the client and controlled trust files were correctly recorded in the books of account in a manner complying with Part D SAR.					
(f) Extraction of client ledger balances for clients and controlled trusts:	Yes	No	Yes	No	
(i)　The extraction of client ledger balances for clients and controlled trusts has been checked for no fewer than two separate dates in the period subject to this report.					
(ii)　The total liabilities to clients and controlled trusts as shown by such ledger accounts has been compared to the cash account balance(s) at each of the separate dates selected in (f)(i) above and agreed.					
(iii)　The cash account balance(s) at each of the dates selected has/have been reconciled to the balance(s) in client bank account and elsewhere as confirmed directly by the relevant banks and building societies.					
(g) Reconciliations:	Yes	No	Yes	No	
(i)　During the accounting year under review, reconciliations have been carried out at least every five weeks or, in the case of passbook-operated separate designated client accounts for controlled trust money, every fourteen weeks.					
(ii)　Each reconciliation is in the form of a statement set out in a logical format which is likely to reveal any discrepancies.					
(iii)　Reconciliation statements have been retained.					
(iv)　On entries in an appropriate sample of reconciliation statements:	Yes	No	Yes	No	
(A)　All accounts containing client money and controlled trust money have been included.					
(B)　All ledger account balances for clients and controlled trusts as at the reconciliation date have been listed and totalled.					
(C)　No debit balances on ledger accounts for clients and controlled trusts have been included in the total.					
(D)　The cash account balance(s) for clients and controlled trusts is/are correctly calculated by the accurate and up to date recording of transactions.					
(E)　The client bank account totals for clients and controlled trusts are complete and correct being calculated by: the closing balance *plus* an accurate and complete list of outstanding lodgments *less* an accurate and complete list of unpresented cheques.					

Results of test checks:

1. For all client money and controlled trust money	Were any breaches discovered? (Tick the appropriate column.)		If 'yes' should breaches be noted in the accountant's report?		Cross references to audit file documentation
(g) Reconciliations:	Yes	No	Yes	No	
(v) Each reconciliation selected under paragraph (iv) above has been achieved by the comparison and agreement *without adjusting or balancing entries* of: total of ledger balances for clients and controlled trusts; total of cash account balances for clients and controlled trusts; total of client bank accounts.					
(vi) In the event of debit balances existing on ledger accounts for clients and controlled trusts, the firm has investigated promptly and corrected the position satisfactorily.					
(vii) In the event of the reconciliations selected under paragraph (iv) above not being in agreement, the differences have been investigated and corrected promptly.					
(h) Payments of client money and controlled trust money:	Yes	No	Yes	No	
Make a test examination of the ledger accounts for clients and controlled trusts in order to ascertain whether payments have been made on any individual account in excess of money held on behalf of that client or controlled trust.					
(i) Office accounts - client money and controlled trust money:	Yes	No	Yes	No	
(i) Check such office ledger and cash account and bank and building society statements as the firm maintains with a view to ascertaining whether any client money or controlled trust money has not been paid into a client account.					
(ii) Investigate office ledger credit balances and ensure that such balances do not include client money or controlled trust money incorrectly held in office account.					
(j) Client money and controlled trust money not held in client account:	Yes	No	Yes	No	
(i) Have sums not held on client account been identified?					
(ii) Has the reason for holding such sums outside client account been established?					
(iii) Has a written client agreement been made if appropriate?					
(iv) Are central records or a central register kept for client money held outside client account on the client's instructions?					
(k) Rule 30 - inter-client transfers	Yes	No	Yes	No	
Make test checks of inter-client transfers to ensure that rule 30 has been complied with.					
(l) Rule 32 (6) - acting for borrower and lender	Yes	No	Yes	No	
Make a test examination of the client ledger accounts in order to ascertain whether rule 32(6) SAR has been complied with, where the firm acts for both borrower and lender in a conveyancing transaction.					
(m) Rule 32(14) - recognised bodies:	Yes	No	Yes	No	
Is a central book of dividend instruction letters kept?					
(n) Information and explanations:	Yes	No	Yes	No	
All information and explanations required have been received and satisfactorily cleared.					

Results of test checks:

2. Liquidators, trustees in bankruptcy, Court of Protection receivers and trustees of occupational pension schemes (rule 9)	Were any breaches discovered? (Tick the appropriate column.)		If 'yes' should breaches be noted in the accountant's report?		Cross references to audit file documentation
	Yes	No	Yes	No	
(a) A record of all bills of costs and written notifications has been maintained which distinguishes profit costs from disbursements, either in the form of a central record or a file of copies of such bills or notifications.					
(b) Records kept under rule 9 including any statements, passbooks and other accounting records originating outside the firm's office have been retained.					
(c) Records kept under rule 9 are kept together centrally, or a central register is kept of the appointments.					

3. Joint accounts (rule 10)	Were any breaches discovered? (Tick the appropriate column.)		If 'yes' should breaches be noted in the accountant's report?		Cross references to audit file documentation
	Yes	No	Yes	No	
(a) A record of all bills of costs and written notifications has been maintained which distinguishes profit costs from disbursements, either in the form of a central record or a file of copies of such bills or notifications.					
(b) Statements and passbooks and/or duplicate statements or copies of passbook entries have been retained.					
(c) Statements, passbooks, duplicate statements and copies of passbook entries are kept together centrally, or a central register of all joint accounts is kept.					

4. Clients' own accounts (rule 11)	Were any breaches discovered? (Tick the appropriate column.)		If 'yes' should breaches be noted in the accountant's report?		Cross references to audit file documentation
	Yes	No	Yes	No	
(a) Statements and passbooks and/or duplicate statements, copies of passbook entries and cheque details have been retained.					
(b) Statements and passbooks and/or duplicate statements, copies of passbook entries and cheque details are kept together centrally, or a central register of clients' own accounts is kept.					

5. Law society guidelines - accounting procedures and systems			
	Yes	No	
Discovery of substantial departures from the guidelines?			*If "yes" please give details below.*

Results of test checks:

6. Please give further details of unsatisfactory items below. *(Please attach additional schedules as required)*

Signature		Date
Reporting Accountant	Print name	

APPENDIX 5

The Law Society

Accountant's Report Form

Every solicitor, registered European lawyer (REL), recognised body, and registered foreign lawyer (RFL) practising in partnership with solicitors or RELs, who holds or receives client money or controlled trust money, or who operates a client's own account as signatory, must produce annually a report by an accountant qualified under rule 37 of the Solicitors' Accounts Rules 1998 to the effect that the solicitor, etc, has complied with Parts A and B, rule 24(1) of Part C, and Part D of the rules. An accountant's report is required from a person who has been held out as a partner in a practice which has held or received client money or controlled trust money. Therefore, any practitioner whose name is included in the list of partners on the firm's letterhead, even if the name appears under a separate heading of 'salaried partner' or 'associate partner', should be included in this report. An accountant's report is also required from a solicitor, REL or RFL who has been a director of a recognised body which is a company, or a member of a recognised body which is a limited liability partnership, if the recognised body has held or received client money or controlled trust money.

When a solicitor or REL retires from practice (or for any reason stops holding or receiving client money or controlled trust money, or operating any client's own account as signatory), he or she is obliged to deliver a report covering the period up to the date on which he or she ceased to hold client money or controlled trust money, or to operate any client's own account as signatory.

Please complete this form in blue ink.
1 Firm Details. *The name of the sole practice, partnership, recognised body or in-house practice for which this report is being submitted. The name(s) under which the office(s) practise(s).*

Firm name(s) during the reporting period		Law Society reference number	

Report Period from		To	

2 Firm's address(es) covered by this report. *All address(es) of the practice must be covered by an accountant's report except offices outside the UK without any solicitors or recognised bodies as principals. Please list on a separate sheet all offices not covered by this report, with reasons.*

Address(es)

Office Type

Office Type

3 **Solicitors, registered European lawyers and registered foreign lawyers covered by this report**. *For a recognised body, this lists the names of all the directors (in the case of a company) or members (in the case of a limited liability partnership), and any other solicitor(s) or registered European lawyer(s) who have held or received client money or controlled trust money, or who have operated any client's own account as signatory.* **Report period**. *This is the period of the report which covers each individual.* **Quote date ceased to hold client money, etc.** *This needs to be completed if the solicitor/registered European lawyer/registered foreign lawyer/ recognised body has ceased to hold client money and/or controlled trust money, and to operate any client's own account as signatory.*

Surname	Initials	Law Society reference No	Status	Report Period From	To	Quote date if ceased to hold client money, etc.

4 Comparison Dates

The results of the comparisons required under rule 42(1)(f) of the Solicitors' Accounts Rules 1998, at the dates selected by me/us were:

(a)   at   [   ]   *(insert date 1)*

     (i)   Liabilities to clients and controlled trusts (and other persons for whom client money is held) as shown by ledger accounts for client and controlled trust matters   £[   ]

     (ii)   Cash held in client account, and client money and controlled trust money held in any account other than a client account, after allowances for lodgments cleared after date and for outstanding cheques   £[   ]

     (iii)   Difference between (i) and (ii) (if any)   £[   ]

(b)   at   [   ]   *(insert date 2)*

     (i)   Liabilities to clients and controlled trusts (and other persons for whom client money is held) as shown by ledger accounts for client and controlled trust matters   £[   ]

     (ii)   Cash held in client account, and client money and controlled trust money held in any account other than a client account, after allowances for lodgments cleared after date and for outstanding cheques   £[   ]

     (iii)   Difference between (i) and (ii) (if any)   £[   ]

Notes:

The figure to be shown in 4(a)(i) and 4(b)(i) above is the total of credit balances, without adjustment for debit balances (unless capable of proper set off, i.e. being in respect of the same client), or for receipts and payments not capable of allocation to individual ledger accounts.

An explanation must be given for any significant difference shown at 4(a)(iii) or 4(b)(iii) - see note (vi) to rule 47 of Solicitors' Accounts Rules 1998. If appropriate, it would be helpful if the explanation is given here.

5 Qualified Report

Have you found it necessary to make this report 'Qualified' ?

No ☐   If 'No' proceed to section 6

Yes ☐   If 'Yes' please complete the relevant boxes

(a)   Please indicate in the space provided any matters (other than trivial breaches) in respect of which it appears to you that the solicitor(s)/registered European lawyer(s)/registered foreign lawyer(s)/ recognised body(ies) has/have not complied with the provisions of Parts A and B, rule 24(1) of Part C, and Part D of the Solicitors' Accounts Rules 1998 and, in the case of private practice only, any part of the period covered by this report (excluding any part of the period falling before 1 September 2000) which in respect of the practice's offices in England and Wales does not appear to have been covered by the certificates or policy of indemnity insurance referred to in rule 42(1)(p) of the Solicitors' Accounts Rules 1998 (*continue on an additional sheet if necessary*):

(b)   Please indicate in the space provided any matters in respect of which you have been unable to satisfy yourself and the reasons for that inability, e.g. because a client's file is not available (*continue on an additional sheet if necessary*):

6 Accountant Details. *The reporting accountant must be qualified in accordance with rule 37 of the Solicitors' Accounts Rules 1998.*

Name

Reference Number

Law Society Use Only

Professional Body   Firm Name

Firm Address

7 Declaration

In compliance with section 34 of the Solicitors Act 1974, schedule 2 paragraph 5(1) of the Administration of Justice Act 1985, schedule 14, paragraph 8 of the Courts and Legal Services Act 1990, and/or schedule 4 paragraph 5(2) of the European Communities (Lawyer's Practice) Regulations 2000 and Part F of the Solicitors' Accounts Rules 1998, I/we have examined to the extent required by rule 42 of those rules, the accounting records, files and other documents produced to me/us in respect of the above practice(s) of the above named solicitor(s)/registered European lawyers(s)/registered foreign lawyers(s)/recognised body(ies).

In so far as an opinion can be based on this limited examination I am/we are satisfied that during the above mentioned period he/she/the body has/they have complied with the provisions of Parts A and B, rule 24(1) of Part C, and Part D of the Solicitor's Accounts Rules 1998 except so far as concerns:

     (i)   certain trivial breaches due to clerical errors or mistakes in book-keeping, all of which were rectified on discovery and none of which, I am/we are satisfied, resulted in any loss to any client or controlled trust; and/or

     (ii)   any matters detailed in section 5 of this report.

In the case of private practice only, I/we certify that, in so far as can be ascertained from a limited examination of the certificates or policy produced to me/us, the practice was covered in respect of its offices in England and Wales for the period covered by this report (excluding any part of the period falling before 1 September 2000) by the certificates or policy of indemnity insurance referred to in rule 42(1)(p) of the Solicitors' Accounts Rules 1998, except as stated in section 5 of this report.

I/we have relied on the exception contained in rule 42(2) of the Solicitors' Accounts Rules 1998

Rule 42(2) of the Solicitors' Accounts Rules 1998 states: *"For the purposes of paragraph(1)(f) above [extraction of balances] if a solicitor uses a computerised or mechanised system of accounting which automatically produces an extraction of all client ledger balances, the accountant need not check all client ledger balances extracted on the list produced by the computer or machine against the individual records of client ledger accounts, provided the accountant:*

(a)   *confirms that a satisfactory system of control is in operation and the accounting records are in balance;*
(b)   *carries out a test check of the extraction against the individual records; and*
(c)   *specifies in the report that he or she has relied on this exception."*

In carrying out work in preparation of this report, I/we have discovered the following substantial departures from the Law Society's current Guidelines for Accounting Procedures and Systems (*continue on an additional sheet if necessary*):

Please tick the 'yes' or 'no' box for the following items (i) to (v) to show whether, so far as you are aware, the relevant statement applies in respect of yourself or any principal, director (in the case of a company), member (in the case of a limited liability partnership) or employee of your accountancy practice. *Give details if appropriate.*

		Yes	No
(i)	Any of the parties mentioned above is related to any solicitor(s)/registered European lawyer(s)/registered foreign lawyer(s) to whom this report relates.		
(ii)	Any of the parties mentioned above normally maintained, on a regular basis, the accounting records to which this report relates.		
(iii)	Any of the parties mentioned above, or the practice, places substantial reliance for referral of clients on the solicitor(s)/registered European lawyers(s)/registered foreign lawyers(s)/ recognised body(ies) to whom/which this report relates.		
(iv)	Any of the parties mentioned above, or the practice, is a client or former client of the solicitor(s)/registered European lawyers(s)/registered foreign lawyers(s)/recognised body(ies) to whom/which this report relates.		
(v)	There are other circumstances which might affect my independence in preparing this report.		

The information is intended to help the Law Society to identify circumstances which might make it difficult to give an independent report. Answering 'yes' to any part of this section does not disqualify the accountant from making the report.

Information within the accountant's personal knowledge should always be disclosed. Detailed investigations are not necessary but reasonable enquiries should be made of those directly involved in the work.

I/we have completed and signed the Law Society checklist and retained a copy. The original checklist has been sent to:

_____ (sole principal, partner (if a partnership), director (if a company), member (if a limited liability partnership))

I/we confirm that a copy of this report has been sent to (* delete as appropriate)

(a)   * Each of the solicitor(s)/registered European lawyers(s)/registered foreign lawyers(s) to whom this report relates; or

(b)   * The following partner of the firm, on behalf of all the partners in the firm:

_____

(c)   * Each of the directors (in the case of a company)/* Each of the members (in the case of a limited liability partnership) of the recognised body to which this report relates; or

(d)   * The following officer of the recognised body (in the case of a company)/* The following member of the recognised body (in the case of a limited liability partnership), on behalf of the recognised body:

_____

The form should then be signed and dated. The report can be signed in the name of the firm of accountants of which the accountant is a partner (in the case of a partnership) or director (in the case of a company) or member (in the case of a limited liability partnership) or employee. Particulars of the individual accountant signing the report must be given in section 6

Date _____

Signature _____

Name (Block Capitals) _____

Please return this form to: Registration, The Law Society, Ipsley Court, Berrington Close, Redditch , Worcestershire, B98 0TD (DX 19114 Redditch)

INDEX TO THE SOLICITORS' ACCOUNTS RULES 1998

This index does not form part of the Rules.

References are to the numbers of the Rules. An 'n' after the Rule number refers to one of the notes appended to that Rule. References to the appendices are prefaced by 'app.'.

Building society balances, confirmation direct to reporting accountant, 42(1)(f)(ii), 42n(iii)

Building society statements, retention, 32(9)(b)–(c), 32(15)

Cash

immediate payment in execution of trust, 18(a)
not passing through client account, 32n(iii)
paid direct to client or third party, 17(a)
withheld from client account on instructions, 16(1)(a)

Central records, 32(8), 32(11)–(14)

Central registers, accounting records

client's own accounts, 33(2)
for instruction letters for dividend payments, 32(14)
for joint accounts, 32(13)
for liquidators, trustees in bankruptcy, Court of Protection receivers or trustees of occupational pension schemes, 32(12)
for money held outside a client account, 32(11)

Certificates of interest, 28

Cessation of partnerships, accounting periods, 36n(ii)

Changes

accounting period, 36(4)
membership of partnerships, accounting periods, 36n(i)
reporting accountant, 38(1)(ii), 39

CHAPS terminals, withdrawal from client account, 23n(i)

Checklist, reporting accountant's, 46, app.4

Checks and tests

accountant's reports, 42
checklist, reporting accountant's, 46, app.4
not required in accountant's reports, 44

Cheques

agreement with banks etc. to retain, 32(10)(a)
blank, 23n(ii), app.3 (para. 5.7)
crossed, 23n(iv)
digital images, 32(10)
endorsed over to client or employer, 13n(ii), 35n(viii)
endorsed over to client or third party, 17(b), 32n(iii)
endorsement methods, 17(n)(iii), 18(n)(iii)
held to sender's order, 13n(v)(b)
immediate endorsement in execution of trust, 18(b), 18(n)(ii)
made payable to client, 32n(iii)
not passing through client account, 32n(iii)
payable to banks, 22n(iv)
received by recognised bodies, 31(2), 32(9)(f)
retention, 32(10)
    of originals, 32(15)(c)
uncleared, 22n(v)
withdrawal in favour of solicitor from client accounts, 23(3)

Clearly identifiable, meaning, 32n(vii)

Client, meaning, 2(2)(e)

Client accounts, 14

 accounting records, 32
 advance from solicitor, 15(2)(b)
 assistant solicitors, 35n(vi)–(vii)
 bank accounts, 14(4)(a)
 building society accounts, 14(4)(b)
 cheques blank, 23n(ii), app.3 (para. 5.7)
 cheques cancelled, app.3 (para. 5.7)
 cheques unused, app.3 (para. 5.7)
 client money withheld, 17
 client money withheld on client's instructions, 16
 consultants, 35n(vi)–(vii)
 controlled trust money withheld, 18
 costs, 19
 interest earned on general client account, 15(2)(d)
 interest earned on money held in, 24
 location, 14(4)
 master list to be maintained, app.3 (para. 5.3)
 meaning, 14(2)
 money to replace sum withdrawn in breach, 15(2)(c)
 naming of client account, 14(3)
 overdrawn, 22(8)
 proper use of, not providing banking facilities, 15n(ix)
 provision of details to reporting accountant, 41
 recognised bodies, 31(1)
 section 85, Solicitors Act 1974, 14n(vi)
 share accounts, 14(4)(b)
 signatory on, 23(1)–(2)
  assistant solicitors and consultants, 35n(vi)
 test procedures, 42
 titles, 14(3)
 use, 15
 withdrawals, 22
  authorisation of Law Society, 22(1)(h), 22(2)(h)
  internal authority, 23
  office money, 22(3), 23(3)
 Wood and Burdett, 15n(ix)
 see also Separate designated client accounts

Client money

 accounting records, 32
 administrative charges, 24n(vi)
 availability, 25n(v)
 duty to replace, 7
 foreign currency, 32n(xiii)
 held for Legal Services Commission, 24(3)(d), 21n(vi)
 held for payment of counsel's fees, 24(3)(c)
 held outside client accounts, 16, 32(11), 42(1)(j)
 immediate payment into client account, 15(1)
 interest, 24, 25
  small amounts, 24(3)(a)
  test procedures, 42(1)(o)

joint accounts, 10n
meaning, 13(a), 13n(i)–(vii), 13n(xii), app.1
mixed payments, 20
provision of details to reporting accountant, 41
receipt of costs, 19
safety, 1(c)
small amounts, waiver of accountant's report, 35n(ix), 49
test procedures, 42
use, 1(d), 22(8)
withdrawals from client accounts, 22
    authorisation of Law Society, 22(1)(h), 22(2)(h)
    in favour of solicitor, 22(3), 23(3)
    internal authority, 23
withheld from client account, 16, 17
see also Person funding solicitor's fees

Client privilege

documents withheld from accountant, 45
overridden by Law Society, 34n(ii)

Client's instructions

master list to be maintained, app.3, (para. 5.3)
withdrawal from client account, 22(1)(e), 22n(vii)
withholding client money from client account, 16, 32(9)(d), app.2

Client's own account

accounting records, 33
master list, to be maintained, app.3 (para.5.3)
opened by solicitor, not operated by solicitor, 16(1)(b), app.2
operation by solicitor, 11
    cessation, 33(3)
operation for limited purpose, 11(4)
power of attorney, 11
provision of details to reporting accountant, 41
record-keeping, 33
shared operation, 11(3)
sole operation, 11(2)
test procedures, 42(1)(n)

Commissions, client money, 13n(i)(e)

Compensation Fund, contributions to, in-house solicitors, 14n(ii)

Compliance with rules

by non-solicitor staff, 4n(i)
by solicitors who cease to hold client money, 4n(ii)
client's own account, operation by solicitor, 11
co-operation with Law Society, 1(i)
Court of Protection receivers, 9
donee under power of attorney, 11
joint accounts, 10
liquidators, 9
monitoring by Law Society, 34
principals' responsibilities, 6, app.3 (para. 5.4(5))
trustees in bankruptcy, 9
trustees of occupational pension schemes, 9

Compound interest, 25n(iv)

Computerised accounting systems, 32(15), app.3 (paras. 2.6–2.7)

    extraction of balances, 42(2)

Confidentiality

    accountant's reports, 38(1)

    overridden by Law Society, 34n(ii)

Confirmation direct to reporting accountant, bank and building society statements, 42(1)(f)(ii), 42n(iii)

Consultants

    accountant's reports, 35n(vi)–(vii)

    application of rules to, 4(1)(a)(iii)

    practice acts for, 13n(xii)(c)

Contracting out

    interest provisions, 24(3)(f), 27

    interest on stakeholder money, 27(2), 27n(ii)–(v)

Controlled trust, meaning, 2(2)(h), 2n(iv)

Controlled trust money

    accounting records, 1(g), 32(1)(b), 32(2), 32(3)(b)

    duty to replace, 7

    foreign currency, 32n(xiii)

    immediate payment into client account, 15(1)

    interest, 15n(vi), 24(7), 24n(x)

    intervention by OSS, 13n(viii)

    meaning, 13(b), 13n(i), 13n(vii)(a), app.1, app.2

    mixed payments, 20

    overdrawing, 22(8)(a)

    paid into another client account, 22(2)(d)

    provision of details to reporting accountant, 41

    recognised bodies, 31(2)

    reconciliations, 32(7)

        passbook-operated accounts, 32(7)

    refund of solicitor's advance, 22(2)(f)

    separate designated account, not used for other payments, 22(7)

    test procedures, 42

    treatment, 8, 15, 18

    use, 1(e), 22(2)

    withdrawals from client account, 22(2)

    withdrawal from general client account, when money held in separate designated account, 22(6)

    withdrawal not to exceed balance, 22(5)

    withheld from client account, 18, app.2

        master list, to be maintained, app.3 (para. 5.3)

Controlled trustees

    assistant solicitor, 35n(vii)

    central register, 32(11)

    consultant, 35n(vii)

    delivery of accountant's reports, 35

Endorsing cheques *see* Cheques

Enduring power of attorney *see* Power of attorney

Estate agents, fees, 2n(v)

European authorised institution, meaning, 2n(iii)

Executors
> meaning, 2(2)(y)
> recognised bodies, 31n(ii)

Exemption from rules, 5, 35n(ii), app.2
> *see also* Accountant's reports, delivery

Experts' fees, 2(2)(s), 2n(v)

Fees
> bill of costs, 19(2), 32(8)
> counsel, 2(2)(s), 24(3)(c)
> court, 13n(i)(c), 19(1)(a)(iii)
> estate agents, 2n(v)
> experts, 2(2)(s), 2n(v)
> interpreters, 2n(v)
> Land Registry fees, 13n(i)(c), 19(1)(a)(iii), 19n(ii), 22n(ii)
> meaning, 2(2)(l)
> money received by solicitor, 19(1)
> process servers, 2n(v)
> search, 19n(ii), 22n(ii)
> surveyors, 2n(v)
> telegraphic transfer, 13n(i)(c), 19(1)(a)(iii)
> translators, 2n(v)
> travel agents, 2n(v)
> *see also* Agreed fees; Costs

Fees due to practice, office money, 13n(xi)(c)(A)

Fellow of the Institute of Legal Executives, authority for withdrawal from client
> account, 23(1)(b)

Financial Services and Markets Act 2000, 15n(ix)

First report, accounting periods, 36(2)

Flow chart, effect of rules, app.1

Foreign currency, client money or controlled trust money, 32n(xiii)

Franchised firms, payments for legal aid work, 21n(ii)

Frequency of updating accounting records, 32n(i)

General client account
> interest, 24(2)–(6)
> interest earned, office money, 13n(xi)(b)
> meaning, 14(5)(b)
> rate of interest, 25
> sum in lieu of interest
>> checks not required in accountant's reports, 44(d)
>> paid into client account, 15(2)(d)

Intermittent sums, money held in client accounts, 24(4)

Internal controls, 1(f), 29, app.3

Interpreters, fees, 2n(v)

Intervention, OSS, money in practice, 13n(viii)

Investigations by Law Society, 34

Investments, 15n(vii), 22(2)(a)
  see also Shares

Joining a partnership, accounting periods, 36n(i)

Joint accounts, 10
  client money, 10n, app.1, app.2
  compliance, 10
  deposit interest, 24n(ix)
  master list, to be maintained, app.3 (para. 5.3)
  production of accounting records, 10(1)(d), 34
  record-keeping, 32(9)(b)(ii), 32(13), 32n(ii)(b)
  register of joint accounts, 32(13)
  test procedures, 42(1)(m)
  with lay trustee, 13n(iv)

Land Registry
  registration fees, client money, 13n(i)(c), 19(1)(a)(iii)
  search fees, 19n(ii), 22n(ii)

Law Society
  authorisation of withdrawal from client account, 22(1)(h), 22(2)(h), 22n(viii)–(ix)
  authority to withhold money from client account, 17(f), 17n(iv), 18(d), 18n(iv)
  guidelines for accounting systems, 29, app.3
  interest certificates, 28
  monitoring of compliance, 34
  see also Office for the Supervision of Solicitors

Leaving a partnership, accounting periods, 36n(i)

Ledger postings, test procedures, 42(1)(b)

Legal Aid Board, 21n(vi)
  see also Legal Services Commission

Legal aid practitioners
  franchised firms, 21n(ii)
  legal aid money in office account, 21(1)(b), 32n(v)
  payments from Legal Services Commission, 19(1)(d), 21(1), 21(2), 21n(vi)
  payments from third parties, 21(3)
  previous solicitor's costs, money received from third party, 21n(v)

Legal Services Commission
  accounting records, 32n(v)
  interest, 24(3)(d)
  Legal Aid Board, 21n(vi)
  payments to legal aid practitioners, 19(1)(d), 21(1), 21(2), 21n(vi)
  settlement by third party, 21(3)

Letter of engagement, accountants, 38

Licensed conveyancers, withdrawal from client account, 23(1)(c)

Lien, solicitor's right against money in client account, 12

Limited Liability Partnerships *see* Recognised bodies

Liquidators

client money, 13n(i)(a), app.1, app.2
compliance with rules, 9, 24n(viii)
record-keeping, 32(9)(c), 32n(ii)(a)
register of appointments, 32(12)
retention of accounting records, 32(9)(c)
test procedures, 42(1)(l)
use of client accounts, 9(3)

Loan *see* Private loans

Local authority, meaning, 5n(ii)

Location, client accounts, 14(4)

Location of examination, books of account, 34(1), 40

Locum, application of rules to, 4(1)(a)(iii)

Manual accounting system, app.3 (para. 2.6)

Mechanised accounting systems

test procedures, 42(2)
see also Computerised accounting systems

Member of limited liability partnership (recognised body)

accountant's reports, 35n(va)
application of rules to, 4(1)(a)(vi)
practice acts for, 13n(xii)(c)
see also Recognised bodies

Misconduct, employees, 4n(i)

Mistakes, accounts, 47n(iv)–(v)

Mixed money, treated as client money, 32n(iv)

Mixed payments

legal aid practitioners, 21(1)(b), 21n(iii)
meaning, 20(1)
receipt and transfer, 20(2)–(5)
receipt from Legal Services Commission, 20(5), 21n(vi)

Money

held for stamp duty, 13n(i)(c)
held in client accounts
aggregation, 15n(viii)
availability, 14n(vii), 25n(v)
held in personal capacity, app.1
held or received by solicitor, app.1

Office accounts

Office for the Supervision of Solicitors

Office money

Outside managers

Paid disbursements

Partnerships

Special situations chart, app.2

Spent, meaning, 22n(ii)

Stakeholder

administrative charges, 27n(ii)–(iv)
contracting out of interest rules, 27(2), 27n(ii)–(v)
holding client money, 13n(i)(a), app.1
interest, 26

Stamp duty

client money, 13n(i)(c)
included with payment of costs, 19(1)(a)(iii)

Standard monthly payments from Legal Services Commission, legal aid practitioners,
21(2), 21n(vii)–(x)

Standard terms of business

client money held outside client account, 16(2)
contracting out by, 27n(i)

Statutory rules

accounting records, 9, 32(9)(c), 32(12), 32(15)(b), 32n(ii)(a)
interest, 24n(viii)

Statutory undertakers

exempt from rules, 5(a)(ii)
meaning, 5n(i)

Stocks, checks not required in accountant's reports, 44(b)

Successive accounts, amount of interest, 25(3)

Sum in lieu of interest, 24(2)–(5), 24(6)(b)

amount of interest, 25
checks not required by reporting accountant, 44(d)
interest certificates, 28
payment into client account, 15(2)(d)
relevant period, 25(2), 25n(i)–(ii)
stakeholder money, 26
when to account to client, 25n(i)

Surveyors, fees, 2n(v)

Suspense ledger accounts, 32(16)

Taxi fares, 19n(ii), 22n(ii)

Telegraphic transfer

calculation of interest, 25n(iii)
for payment of costs, 19n(vi)–(viii)
not received, 22n(vi)

Telegraphic transfer fees

client money, 13n(i)(c)
included with payment of costs, 19(1)(a)(iii)

Telephone instructions, withdrawal from client account, 23n(i)

Test procedures, accountant's reports, 42

Annex C

Guidance – transitional arrangements for the delivery of accountants' reports

---

[The transitional period has now ended, so this annex is no longer applicable and has been deleted]

Annex D

Tax on bank and building society interest – practice information

Since April 1996, savings income received by an individual, the estate of a deceased person or an interest in possession trust has been taxable at the lower rate (20%), unless in the case of an individual his or her total income makes him or her liable to higher rate tax, rather than the basic rate of tax (section 73 of the Finance Act 1996 inserting a new section 1A into the Income and Corporation Taxes Act 1988). This is relevant to the tax treatment of bank and building society interest received by solicitors.

The Solicitors' Accounts Rules 1998, Part C

Under this part of the rules ('the interest provisions'), a solicitor who is required to account for interest to a client may do so by either of two methods. He or she may:

(a) account to the client for the interest earned on the client's money in a separate designated client account; or

(b) pay to the client a sum in lieu of interest when the money is held in a general client account.

These two procedures are referred to as Method A and Method B respectively.

Deduction of tax at source

The tax deduction at source rules apply, broadly, to separate designated client accounts, e.g. accounts held for individuals who are ordinarily resident in the U.K.

Interest on general client accounts, whether with a bank or a building society, is paid gross.

When opening any separate designated client account the solicitor must provide the necessary information for the bank or building society to decide whether or not deduction of tax at source is appropriate.

Tax treatment of interest – Method A

Method A applies to separate designated client accounts. Where tax is deducted at source by the bank or building society interest will be received by the solicitor net, and he or she will simply pass it on to the client net – no tax deduction certificate is required. Interest from separate designated client accounts is taxable as savings income. The client, when making his or her tax return, will declare the interest as having been received under deduction of tax, and will only be liable to be assessed in relation to higher rate tax in respect of it (since he or she will have a tax credit for the lower rate of tax). If the client is for any reason not liable to income tax, he or she can recover any tax deducted from the interest. In those circumstances the solicitor must, on being required by the client, obtain a certificate of deduction of tax from the bank or building society and deliver this to the client. The client's position is, therefore, for practical purposes, the same as that which arises where he or she receives interest from a building society or bank on a deposit of his or her own.

Where the client is not liable to tax or is not ordinarily resident (NOR) in the U.K. the bank or building society will pay the interest gross provided that it holds the relevant declaration. Declarations of non-ordinary residence can be completed by either the solicitor or the client but declarations of non-liability by U.K. residents will normally be completed by the client. However, in view of the difficulty of obtaining complete information about an overseas client, solicitors may feel that it is more appropriate for the client concerned to make the declaration, especially since it contains an undertaking to notify the bank or building society should circumstances change.

Where the tax deduction at source rules do not apply, the solicitor will receive interest from the bank or building society gross and may account to the client for it gross, even if the client is non-resident. The client will be assessed on the gross receipt (but a non-resident client may, by concession, not be assessed) and (unless the solicitor has been acting as the client's agent for tax purposes – see below under 'Solicitors as agents') the solicitor himself or herself will not be assessed in respect of the interest.

Tax treatment of interest – Method B

Where Method B is used, deduction of tax at source does not apply to the solicitor's general client account at either a bank or building society, and interest is therefore paid to the solicitor gross. When making a payment to the client of a sum in lieu of interest under the interest provisions, the solicitor should make the payment gross even if the client is not ordinarily resident. The Revenue's view is that such payments may be treated as within Case III of Schedule D, so that the lower rate of tax on savings income may apply where appropriate. The client will be assessed to income tax on his or her receipt, but a non-resident may, by concession, not be assessed.

Wherever payments are made by solicitors to clients under Method B they can, in practice, be set off against the solicitor's Case III assessment on gross interest received on general client account deposits; if the payments exceed the interest received, a Case II deduction can be claimed for the excess.

Stake money

Since 1st June 1992, stake money has been included in the definition of 'client money'. Interest will be payable to the person to whom the stake is paid using either Method A or B above. But there will still be circumstances in which payment is not possible until a later tax year. Where this situation looks likely to arise, e.g. if the stake is held pending the outcome of litigation, the deposit would normally be placed in a general client account until it is established to whom the stake is to be paid. Because, in the meantime, interest will be included in the solicitor's Case III assessment, it is again important to make provision for the tax liability to be met out of the interest as it arises.

Tax treatment of interest – money paid into court

The position of money paid into court is covered by the Supreme Court Funds Rules as amended. Where any order for payment out of money paid into court is made, the order should provide for the disposal of any interest accrued to the date of the judgment or order, and for interest accruing thereafter up to the date the money is paid out in accordance with the order. In the absence of such provision, interest accruing between the date of the payment into court, and its acceptance or the judgment or order for payment out, goes to the party who made the payment in, and interest from the date of the judgment or order follows the capital payment.

Where interest is paid to a party to proceedings in respect of money held in court, it should be paid to the client gross, even if he or she is non-resident. The client will normally be assessable under Case III, but the solicitor will not, unless exceptionally he or she is assessable as the client's agent.

Solicitors as agents

Where a solicitor acts for tax purposes as agent for a non-resident client, the solicitor will remain liable to be assessed on behalf of the client in relation to interest earned in a separate designated client account, where Method A is used, unless he or she is an agent without management or control of the interest, in which case, under Extra Statutory Concession B13, no assessment will be made on him or her. Where the solicitor is assessable, the charge may, if appropriate, be to higher rate tax, so the solicitor will need to retain tax at the client's marginal rate of income tax from interest received gross from a bank or building society before remitting it to the client. This is the case even though the account would not be subject to deduction of tax at source since the client would have completed a declaration of non-liability due to his or her non-residence. No question of the solicitor being taxed as an agent will arise where the interest in question has been earned in a general client account, or on stake money, but it could very exceptionally do so in relation to money held in court.

Determination of whether a solicitor has management or control for the purposes of the extra statutory concession will depend on the nature of the solicitor's relationship with the client. Under the Finance Act 1995, a person not resident in the U.K. is assessable and chargeable to income tax in the name of an agent if the agent has management or control of the interest. Acting as a solicitor in giving advice or in conducting a transaction on the client's instructions will not of itself give management or control nor usually would the holding of a power of attorney on behalf of the client for a specific purpose, e.g. concluding a specified purchase or sale. If a client had no fixed place of business in the U.K., and his or her solicitor had, and habitually exercised, an authority to conclude contracts on behalf of the client, this would give rise to the client having a permanent establishment in the U.K., and accordingly the client would be taxable. In essence, the solicitor would be deemed to have management and control if he or she were effectively carrying on the client's business in the U.K., rather than merely acting as a solicitor, even regularly. Therefore, in order for the agency principle to apply, the solicitor/client relationship would normally have to go beyond a solicitor's usual representative capacity. It should be noted that where interest arises in connection with the receipt of rents on behalf of the non-resident, the solicitor would be chargeable as agent in relation to the rent.

For a more detailed analysis of when solicitors can be taxed as agents, see [1991] *Gazette,* 1 May, 15 (article by John Avery Jones).

If a solicitor is assessable on behalf of the client, he or she has a general right to reimbursement, out of the client's money coming into his or her hands, for any tax for which the client is liable and in respect of which the solicitor has been charged. For the exercise of this right see the Finance Act 1995.

Trusts

Deduction of tax at source may apply depending upon the type of trust and where the investment is held. But it can only apply where money is held in a separate designated client account. The income of trusts where none of the beneficiaries is ordinarily resident in the U.K. will not be subject to deduction of tax at source, even if a separate designated client account is used, provided that the appropriate declaration has been made.

Administration of estates

Interest on money held for U.K. resident personal representatives will, if placed in a separate designated client account, be subject to deduction of tax at source unless a declaration is made by the solicitor or the personal representatives that the deceased was not resident in the U.K. immediately before his death.

AIDE-MEMOIRE OF NORMAL SITUATIONS

Type of account	Payment of interest by bank or building society	Consequences
A Designated – where subject to tax deduction	Net	Pay net to client, who gets basic rate tax credit. No further tax deductions for residents (unless solicitor is assessable as an agent).
B Designated – where paid gross (client money generally)	Gross	Pay gross to client who is assessable on payment as gross income. No deduction of tax for non-residents (unless the solicitor is assessable as agent).
C Bank and building society general client account – always paid gross (client money generally and stake money)	Gross	Pay gross to client who in turn is assessable on payment as gross income; in practice solicitor assessed on interest after setting-off this payment. No deduction of tax for non-residents.

4th March 1992, revised February 1999

Annex E

Treatment of VAT on counsel's fees – practice information

_____

The 1991 accounts rules provided that unpaid counsel's fees should be paid into and kept in client account, rather than in office account as was possible under the previous rules. The 1998 rules allow unpaid counsel's fees to be held temporarily in office account for a short period before payment or transfer to client account.

This has raised the question of how the solicitor should deal with the VAT element on such fees.

Unpaid counsel's fees paid into and kept in client account

The position with regard to VAT on counsel's fees paid into and kept in client account is that by concession of the Customs and Excise, solicitors may either:

Method (i)

treat the fee as their own expense (and thus reclaim the VAT element as input tax);

or

Method (ii)

cross out their name on the receipted fee note and replace it with the name of the client. In this case the supply is deemed to be made direct to the client (who can reclaim the VAT if registered) and no VAT record need be kept in the solicitor's books.

If method (i) is used, when the solicitor delivers his own bill of costs, the value of the supply for VAT purposes is the value of his or her own costs, plus the tax exclusive value of counsel's fees. Thus in this case the solicitor is charging output tax on a higher level of supply.

The following examples show the effect of the two methods:

Assume solicitor's profit costs as £1,200 plus £210 VAT and the bill includes unpaid counsel's fees of £800, plus £140 VAT:

Method (i)

The £140 VAT on counsel's fee note is treated as the solicitor's input tax and can be reclaimed from Customs and Excise. When the solicitor's bill is delivered it must show:

Value of supply:	
Costs	1,200.00
Counsel's fees	800.00
	————
	£2,000.00
VAT	350.00
	————
	£2,350.00
	————

When the £2,350 is received, the effect of the accounts rules is that the cheque must either be split, sending the office element (£1,200 costs and £350 VAT) to office account and counsel's fees to client account (£800), or alternatively the entire sum of £2,350 must be paid into client account.

Because counsel's fee is being treated for VAT purposes as an expense of the solicitor and the VAT element is being reclaimed by the solicitor, payment, when it is made, must be from office account (so that the appropriate entry can be made in the Customs and Excise ledger account). At that stage the sum held in client account can be transferred.

Method (ii)

The solicitor will simply deliver a bill showing no book-keeping entries for the counsel's fees and VAT. It will simply show:

Profit costs	1,200.00
VAT	210.00
	————
	£1,410.00
Counsel's fees	
(including VAT)	940.00
	————
	£2,350.00

The effect of the accounts rules is that the cheque must either be split as to £1,410 office account and £940 client account, or alternatively the entire sum of £2,350 must be paid into client account. In this case, when counsel is paid payment can be made from either client or office account (with a subsequent transfer to office account from client account).

Placing and holding unpaid counsel's fees temporarily in office account

Solicitors who use the new option, under the 1998 Accounts Rules, of placing unpaid counsel's fees initially in office account, would be unable to treat the supply as being made direct to the client. The office account should not, therefore, be used for unpaid counsel's fees if the intention is to take advantage of the concessionary treatment and treat the supply as being made direct to the client.

September 1992, revised February 1999

Annex F

Solicitors' Overseas Practice Rules 1990 (extracts)

(with consolidated amendments to 17th March 2004)

Rules dated 18th July 1990 made by the Council of the Law Society with the concurrence, where requisite, of the Master of the Rolls under Part II of the Solicitors Act 1974 and section 9 of the Administration of Justice Act 1985, regulating

- *the practices of solicitors and recognised bodies outside England and Wales, and*
- *the practices of registered European lawyers in Scotland and Northern Ireland.*

Rule 1 – Ambit of the rules

(1)   These rules shall apply to all forms of practice of a solicitor of the Supreme Court and to a recognised body incorporated in England and Wales.

(2)   Subject always to any requirements of the relevant law or of such local rules as may be applicable to him or her, a solicitor of the Supreme Court practising as such from an office outside England and Wales, or a recognised body incorporated in England and Wales and practising from an office outside England and Wales, shall in respect of that practice comply with these rules and not be subject to any other rules made by the Council under sections 31, 32, 33A, 34 or 37 of the Act or section 9 of the Administration of Justice Act 1985 except where it is expressly provided to the contrary in any such rules or in these rules.

(2A) A recognised body incorporated outside England and Wales and practising from an office outside England and Wales shall not, in respect of that practice, be subject to these rules or any other rules made by the Council under sections 31, 32, 33A, 34 or 37 of the Act or section 9 of the Administration of Justice Act 1985 except where it is expressly provided to the contrary in these rules, and subject always to any requirements of the relevant law or of such local rules as may be applicable to the recognised body.

(3)   These rules shall also apply, on the basis set out in paragraphs (1) and (2) of this rule, to registered European lawyers practising in Scotland or Northern Ireland.

(4)   A solicitor of the Supreme Court, or a registered European lawyer, practising from an office outside England and Wales and acting as an advocate in England and Wales on a visiting basis shall comply with the Law Society's Code for Advocacy.

(5)   The Solicitors' Financial Services (Scope) Rules, the Solicitors' Financial Services (Conduct of Business) Rules and Rule 12 (investment business) of the Solicitors' Practice Rules apply to the practices in any part of the world of solicitors of the Supreme Court and recognised bodies (whether incorporated in England and Wales or outside England and Wales), and the practices in any part of the United Kingdom of registered European lawyers, in the conduct of investment business in, into or from the United Kingdom.

Explanatory notes

(i)   These rules are not an exhaustive statement of the professional obligations of solicitors practising outside England and Wales. The Council considers that the principles of professional conduct which apply in England and Wales apply to all solicitors, even where no specific reference to a particular principle appears in these rules. For example, although these rules do not include any equivalent of Rule 10 of the Solicitors' Practice Rules (receipt of commissions from third parties), the general principle that a solicitor must account to his or her client for any commission or secret profit still applies. Similarly, a solicitor must not act in any situation where he or she would be involved in a conflict of interest.

(ii)   The Solicitors' Compensation Fund Rules, made under section 36 of the Act, apply to practices outside England and Wales; these are not rules of conduct, but relate to the Solicitors' Compensation Fund and procedures for making grants from it.

(iii)   Paragraph (2A) does not remove the obligation of a solicitor of the Supreme Court (or in Scotland or Northern Ireland a registered European lawyer) practising through a recognised body incorporated outside England and Wales, or in the employment of such a body, to comply with the Overseas Practice Rules.

(iv)   For the application of various rules under paragraphs (2) and (2A), see also Rule 9(2)(a) and (b), and Rule 9(3)(e).

(v)   As an example of local rules being applicable (paragraphs (2) and (2A)), a solicitor of the Supreme Court who is established in a host state under the Establishment of Lawyers Directive 98/5/EC is subject to local rules by virtue of Article 6 of the Directive. The solicitor remains subject to the Law Society's rules also – unless compliance with a particular requirement is prevented by a provision in the local rules, in which case the local provision will prevail.

Rule 9 – Corporate practice

(1)   A solicitor of the Supreme Court shall not practise outside England and Wales, and a registered European lawyer shall not practise in Scotland or Northern Ireland, through a body corporate, unless:

   (a)   the body corporate is wholly owned and directed by:

      (i)   practising members of legal professions covered by the Establishment of Lawyers Directive 98/5/EC; and/or

      (ii)   practising members of other legal professions (but excluding any whose registration under section 89 of the Courts and Legal Services Act 1990 is suspended or whose name has been struck off the register); or

   (b)   the body corporate is owned and directed by persons within (a) above together with non-lawyers, provided that:

      (i)   a controlling majority of the owners and of the directors are lawyers;

      (ii)   the non-lawyers' involvement in the body does not put the lawyers in breach of any applicable local rules; and

      (iii)   if the body has an office in an Establishment Directive state, the rules applying in that state would permit local lawyers to practise through a body corporate with similar involvement of non-lawyers; or

   (c)   the solicitor or registered European lawyer is employed in-house as permitted by Rule 7 of these rules.

(2)   (a)   All the provisions of the Solicitors' Incorporated Practice Rules shall apply to the practice outside England and Wales of a recognised body incorporated in England and Wales.

     (b)   All the provisions of the Solicitors' Incorporated Practice Rules, except Rule 2(1)(a)(i) (application of principles and requirements of conduct to recognised bodies), shall apply to the practice outside England and Wales of a recognised body incorporated outside England and Wales.

(3)   (a)   Where solicitors of the Supreme Court own a controlling majority of the shares in a corporate practice which is a company with a share capital but is not a recognised body, the provisions of Rules 12 to 16 of these rules shall apply to all solicitors of the Supreme Court who own shares in or are directors of that corporate practice as if all such solicitors and any other owners of shares and directors were practising in partnership as the principals of that practice.

     (b)   Where solicitors of the Supreme Court constitute a controlling majority of the members of a corporate practice which is a company without a share capital but is not a recognised body, the provisions of Rules 12 to 16 shall apply to all solicitors of the Supreme Court who are members or directors of that corporate practice as if all such solicitors of the Supreme Court and any other members and directors were practising in partnership as the principals of that practice.

     (c)   Where solicitors of the Supreme Court constitute a controlling majority of the members of a corporate practice which is a body corporate but is not a company and is not a recognised body, the provisions of Rules 12 to 16 shall apply to all solicitors of the Supreme Court who are members of that corporate practice as if all such solicitors of the Supreme Court and any other members were practising in partnership as the principals of that practice.

     (d)   Where solicitors of the Supreme Court constitute a controlling majority of the partners of a practice which is a partnership with a separate legal identity and which holds funds as such and in which the individual partners are protected from liability for the debts of the partnership, the provisions of Rules 12 to 16 shall apply to all solicitors of the Supreme Court who are partners in that practice as if all such solicitors of the Supreme Court and any other partners were practising as the principals of that practice in a partnership formed under English law.

     (e)   Where solicitors of the Supreme Court:

        (i)   own a controlling majority of the shares in a recognised body incorporated outside England and Wales as a company with a share capital; or

        (ii)   constitute a controlling majority of the members of a recognised body incorporated outside England and Wales as a company without a share capital;

     the provisions of Rules 12 to 16 of these rules shall apply to the recognised body as if it were a recognised body incorporated in England and Wales.

(4)   Solicitors of the Supreme Court who are:

     (a)   shareowners in or directors of a corporate practice falling within paragraph (3)(a) of this Rule; or

(b)   members or directors of a corporate practice falling within paragraph (3)(b); or

(c)   members of a corporate practice falling within paragraph (3)(c);

shall, where the corporate practice holds money as sole trustee or co-trustee only with one or more of its officers or employees (in case (a) or (b) above), or one or more of its members or employees (in case (c) above), be treated for the purposes of Rules 12, 13, 15 and 16 of these rules as holding money subject to a controlled trust.

(5)   In the case of a corporate practice in Scotland or Northern Ireland, "solicitors of the Supreme Court" in paragraphs (3) and (4) of this rule shall be read as including registered European lawyers.

Explanatory notes

(i)   A corporate practice operating both in England and Wales and in another jurisdiction needs to comply, in respect of its overseas practice, both with the Solicitors' Overseas Practice Rules and the Solicitors' Incorporated Practice Rules. A corporate practice operating solely outside England and Wales needs to comply with the Solicitors' Overseas Practice Rules but is not eligible for recognition under the Solicitors' Incorporated Practice Rules.

(ii)   As a result of paragraphs (3)(a) to (c) and (4), the solicitor shareowners and directors (in the case of a company with a share capital), or solicitor members and directors (in the case of a company without a share capital), or solicitor members (in the case of a body corporate which is not a company) must ensure that the corporate practice complies with Rules 12 and/or 13, and 14, in relation to clients' money or controlled trust money, which will be subject to the reporting accountant's check under Rule 16; and these solicitors must ensure that the corporate practice complies with Rule 15 (investigation of accounts) and 15A (general investigations).

Rule 12 – Solicitors' accounts

(1)   (a)   A solicitor shall keep any money held by him or her on behalf of clients separate from any other funds (save as provided in sub-paragraph (1)(d) of this rule) and in an account at a bank or similar institution subject to supervision by a public authority.

(b)   All money received by a solicitor for or on behalf of a client shall be paid into such an account forthwith unless the client expressly or by implication agrees that the money shall be dealt with otherwise.

(c)   Any such account in which clients' money is held in the name of the solicitor shall indicate in the title or designation that the funds belong to the client or clients of the solicitor.

(d)   In such account may be kept money held subject to a controlled trust and paid into such account in accordance with Rule 13(1)(a) of these rules.

(2)   A solicitor shall at all times keep, whether by written, electronic, mechanical or other means, such accounts as are necessary:

(a)   to record all the solicitor's dealings with money dealt with through any such account for clients' money as is specified in sub-paragraph (1)(a) of this rule;

(b)   to show separately in respect of each client all money received, held or paid by the solicitor for or on account of that client and to distinguish the same from any other money received, held or paid by the solicitor; and

(c)   to ensure that the solicitor is at all times able without delay to account to clients for all money received, held or paid by the solicitor on their behalf.

(3)   A solicitor shall not make any payment or withdrawal from money held on behalf of any client except where the money paid or withdrawn is:

(a)   properly required for a payment to or on behalf of the client;

(b)   properly required for or towards payment of a debt due to the solicitor from the client or in reimbursement of money expended by the solicitor on behalf of the client;

(c)   paid or withdrawn on the client's authority; or

(d)   properly required for or towards payment of the solicitor's costs where there has been delivered to the client a bill of costs or other written intimation of the amount of the costs incurred and it has thereby or otherwise in writing been made clear to the client that the money so paid or withdrawn is being or will be so applied.

(4)   A solicitor shall not make any payment or withdrawal from money held subject to a controlled trust and kept in an account in accordance with sub-paragraph (1)(d) of this rule except in proper execution of that trust.

(5)   Every solicitor shall preserve for at least six years from the date of the last entry therein all accounts, books, ledgers and records kept under this rule.

(6)   A solicitor of the Supreme Court practising outside England and Wales is exempt from this rule if:

(a)   the solicitor holds or receives clients' money as a partner in a firm in which a controlling majority of the partners are lawyers of other jurisdictions; and

(b)   UK lawyers do not form the largest national group of lawyers in the partnership.

(7)   In paragraph (6) of this rule, in the case of a practice in Scotland or Northern Ireland, "solicitor of the Supreme Court" shall be read as including a registered European lawyer.

Explanatory notes

(i)   Assistance in the keeping of solicitors' accounts may be derived from the Solicitors' Accounts Rules.

(ii)   Even where local rules applicable to a solicitor may sometimes prevent compliance with some of the provisions of this rule (e.g. the requirements in paragraphs (1) and (2)(a)), it will normally still be possible to comply with other provisions of the rule (e.g. the requirements of paragraphs (2)(b) and (c) and (5)).

Rule 13 – Solicitors' trust accounts

(1)   A solicitor who holds or receives money subject to a controlled trust of which he or she is a trustee shall without delay pay such money either:

(a)   into an account for clients' money such as is specified in Rule 12(1)(a) of these Rules; or

(b)   into an account in the name of the trustee or trustees at a bank or similar institution subject to supervision by a public authority, which account shall be clearly designated as a trust account by use of the words "executor" or "trustee" or otherwise, and shall be kept solely for money subject to that particular trust;

provided that a solicitor shall not be obliged to comply with sub-paragraphs (1)(a) or (b) of this rule where money received is without delay paid straight over to a third party in the execution of the trust.

(2)   A solicitor shall at all times keep, whether by written, electronic, mechanical or other means, such accounts as are necessary:

    (a)   to show separately in respect of each controlled trust all the solicitor's dealings with money received, held or paid by the solicitor on account of that trust; and

    (b)   to distinguish the same from money received or paid by the solicitor on any other account.

(3)   A solicitor shall not make any payment or withdrawal from money held subject to a controlled trust except in proper execution of that trust.

(4)   Every solicitor shall preserve for at least six years from the date of the last entry therein all accounts, books, ledgers and records kept under this rule.

(5)   Every solicitor shall either:

    (a)   keep together, centrally, the accounts required to be kept under this rule; or

    (b)   maintain a central register of controlled trusts.

(6)   A solicitor of the Supreme Court practising outside England and Wales is exempt from this rule if:

    (a)   the solicitor holds or receives controlled trust money as a partner in a firm in which a controlling majority of the partners are lawyers of other jurisdictions; and

    (b)   UK lawyers do not form the largest national group of lawyers in the partnership.

(7)   In paragraph (6) of this rule, in the case of a practice in Scotland or Northern Ireland, "solicitor of the Supreme Court" shall be read as including a registered European lawyer.

Explanatory notes

(i)   Assistance in keeping of trust accounts may be derived from the Solicitors' Accounts Rules.

(ii)   Even where local rules applicable to a solicitor may sometimes prevent compliance with some of the provisions of this rule (e.g. the requirements in paragraph (1)), it will normally still be possible to comply with other provisions of the rule (e.g. the requirements of paragraphs (2), (4) and (5)).

Rule 14 – Deposit interest

Where a solicitor holds or receives for or on behalf of a client money on which, having regard to all the circumstances (including the amount and the length of the time for which the money is likely to be held and the law and prevailing custom of lawyers practising in the jurisdiction in which the solicitor practises) interest ought, in fairness, to be earned for the client, then, subject to any agreement to the contrary made in writing between solicitor and client, the solicitor shall either:

(a)   deal with that money in such a way that proper interest is earned thereon; or

(b)   pay to the client out of the solicitor's own money a sum equivalent to the interest which would have been earned for the benefit of the client had the money been dealt with in accordance with paragraph (a) of this rule.

Rule 15 – Investigation of accounts

(1)   In order to ascertain whether or not Rules 12 to 14 of these rules have been complied with, the Council may at any time in writing (including by telex or facsimile transmission) require any solicitor to produce at a time and place to be fixed by the Council all necessary documents for the inspection of any person appointed by the Council and to supply to such person any necessary information and explanations, and such person shall be directed to prepare a report on the result of such inspection.

(2)   Any requirement made by the Council of a solicitor under paragraph (1) of this rule shall be deemed to have been received by the solicitor upon proof of its having been delivered at or transmitted to the solicitor's practising address or last known practising address (or, in the case of a recognised body, its registered office).

(3)   Upon being required to do so a solicitor shall produce all necessary documents at the time and place fixed, and shall supply any necessary information and explanations.

(4)   Where a requirement is made by the Council of a recognised body under paragraph (1) of this rule such requirement shall, if so stated in the requirement, be deemed also to be made of any solicitor who is an officer or employee of that recognised body (if it is a company), or who is a member or employee of that recognised body (if it is a limited liability partnership), where such solicitor holds or has held client's money or money subject to a controlled trust of which he or she is or was a trustee.

(5)   For the avoidance of doubt, "documents" in paragraph (1) of this rule includes documents, whether written or electronic, relating to the solicitor's client, trust and office accounts.

(6)   The Council's appointee is entitled to seek verification from clients, staff and the banks or similar institutions used by the solicitor. The solicitor must, if necessary, provide written permission for the information to be given.

(7)   Any report made by the Council's appointee may, if appropriate, be sent to the Crown Prosecution Service or the Serious Fraud Office and/or used in proceedings before the Solicitors' Disciplinary Tribunal. In the case of a registered European lawyer, the report may also be sent to the competent authority in the home state or states. In the case of a solicitor of the Supreme Court who is established in another state under the Establishment of Lawyers Directive 98/5/EC, the report may also be sent to the competent authority in the host state. The report may also be sent to any professional body of which a person who has signed an accountant's report under Rule 16 is a member or by which he or she is regulated, and/or taken into account by the Council in relation to a possible disqualification of that person from signing an accountant's report in future.

Rule 15A – General investigations

(1)   Any solicitor must at the time and place fixed by the Law Society produce any documents held by the solicitor or held under the solicitor's control:

(a)   in connection with the solicitor's practice; or

(b)   in connection with any trust of which the solicitor is or formerly was a trustee,

for inspection by a person appointed by the Society for the purpose of ascertaining whether the solicitor is complying with rules 1–11 and 16–18A of these rules, and any other rules, codes or guidance made or issued by the Council of the Law Society with application to overseas practice.

(2)   A requirement for production under paragraph (1) above must be in writing (including by telex or facsimile transmission) and is deemed to have been received by the solicitor upon proof of its having been delivered at or transmitted to the solicitor's practising address or last known practising address (or, in the case of a recognised body, its registered office).

(3)   "Documents" in paragraph (1) of this rule includes documents, whether written or electronic, relating to the solicitor's client, trust and office accounts.

(4)   Documents held electronically must be produced in the form required by the Society's appointee.

(5)   The Council's appointee is entitled to seek verification from clients, staff and the banks or similar institutions used by the solicitor. The solicitor must, if necessary, provide written permission for the information to be given.

(6)   The Society may use any information obtained under this rule in proceedings before the Solicitors' Disciplinary Tribunal and, if the information indicates that the solicitor or an employee of the solicitor (or a director or employee in the case of a company, or a member or employee in the case of a body corporate which is not a company) may have committed a serious criminal offence, may disclose the information for use in investigating the possible commission of a criminal offence and in any subsequent prosecution. In the case of a registered European lawyer, the information may also be sent to the competent authority in the home state or states. In the case of a solicitor of the Supreme Court who is established in another state under the Establishment of Lawyers Directive 98/5/EC, the information may also be sent to the competent authority in the host state.

Rule 16 – Accountants' reports

(1)   The accountant's report which a solicitor is required to deliver annually to the Council under section 34 of the Act (or, in the case of registered European lawyers, paragraph 8 of Schedule 14 to the Courts and Legal Services Act 1990) shall be signed either by a qualified accountant (who may be an accountant qualified in the jurisdiction where the solicitor practises) or by such other person as the Council may think fit.

(2)   Such report shall be based on a sufficient examination of the relevant documents to give the person signing the report a reasonable indication whether or not the solicitor has complied with Rules 12 and 13 of these rules during the period covered by the report.

(3)   Such report shall include:

(a)   the name, practising addresses and practising style of the solicitor and any partners of the solicitor;

(b)   the name, address and qualification of the person signing the report;

(c)   an indication of the nature and extent of the examination made of the relevant documents by the said person;

(d)   a statement to the effect that so far as may be ascertained from the examination the said person is satisfied (if this is indeed the case) that (save for trivial breaches, or situations where the solicitor has been bound by a local rule not to comply) the solicitor has complied with Rules 12 and 13 of these rules during the period covered by the report;

(e) a statement of the total amount of money held at banks or similar institutions on behalf of clients on a date during the period under review, which date shall be selected by the accountant and which may be the last day of the period to which the report relates, and of the total liabilities to clients on such date, and an explanation of any difference; and

(f) details of any matters in respect of which the said person has been unable so to satisfy him or herself and any matters (other than trivial breaches, or situations where the solicitor has been bound by a local rule not to comply) in respect of which it appears to the said person that the solicitor has not complied with Rules 12 and 13 of these rules.

(4) The delivery of an accountant's report shall be unnecessary in respect of any period during which the solicitor was exempt from Rules 12 and 13 or did not hold or receive money for or on behalf of clients or money subject to a controlled trust; except that if a recognised body is required to deliver an accountant's report under these rules, that duty extends also to any solicitor who was a director of the body (if it is a company) or a member of the body (if it is a limited liability partnership) during the relevant accounting period.

(5) It shall be unnecessary to deliver an accountant's report until after the end of any period of twelve months ending 31st October during which the solicitor first held or received money for or on behalf of clients or money subject to a controlled trust, having not held or received any such money in the period of twelve months immediately preceding that period; provided that an accountant's report then delivered includes the period when such money was first held or received.

(6) The Council may for reasonable cause disqualify a person from signing accountant's reports.

Explanatory notes

(i) Assistance in the preparation of accountants' reports may be derived from the Solicitors' Accounts Rules. Reference should also be made to section 34 of the Act.

(ii) Where a firm practises both in England and Wales and overseas, it would, if desired, be proper for a single report to be submitted covering both the "domestic" and overseas parts of the practice.

(iii) In checking controlled trust accounts, the reporting accountant may find it helpful to refer to the series of checks contained in Rule 42(1) of the Solicitors' Accounts Rules and the guidance on test checks on overseas controlled trust accounts in paragraph 28.06 of the 1999 edition of "The Guide to the Professional Conduct of Solicitors".

(iv) For the disqualification of reporting accountants, see also Rule 37 of the Solicitors' Accounts Rules.

Rule 19 – Waivers

In any particular case or cases the Council shall have power to waive in writing any of the provisions of these rules for a particular purpose or purposes expressed in such waiver, and to revoke such waiver.

Rule 20 – Interpretation

In these Rules, except where the context otherwise requires:

(a) the expressions "accounts", "books", "ledgers" and "records" include loose-leaf books and such cards or other permanent documents or records as are necessary for the operation of any system of book-keeping whether written, electronic, mechanical or otherwise;

(b) "the Act" means the Solicitors Act 1974;

(c) "another jurisdiction" means a jurisdiction other than England and Wales;

(d) "controlled trust", in relation to a solicitor of the Supreme Court, or a registered European lawyer practising in Scotland or Northern Ireland, means a trust of which he or she is a sole trustee or co-trustee only with one or more of his or her partners or employees;

(e) "controlled trust", in relation to a recognised body, means a trust of which it is a sole trustee or co-trustee only with one or more of its officers or employees (in the case of a company); or a sole trustee or co-trustee only with one or more of its members or employees (in the case of a limited liability partnership);

(f) [deleted]

(fa) [deleted]

(g) [deleted]

(ga) [deleted]

(h) "the Council" means the Council of the Law Society;

(i) "lawyer", except in Rule 4 of these rules, means a member of a regulated legal profession;

(j) "person" includes a body corporate or unincorporated association or group of persons;

(k) "recognised body" means a body corporate for the time being recognised by the Council under the Solicitors' Incorporated Practice Rules from time to time in force;

(ka) "registered European lawyer" means an individual registered with the Law Society under regulation 17 of the European Communities (Lawyer's Practice) Regulations 2000;

(l) "solicitor" means a solicitor of the Supreme Court and shall also be construed as including a registered European lawyer practising in Scotland or Northern Ireland, and a recognised body incorporated in England and Wales;

(la) "solicitor of the Supreme Court" means an individual who is a solicitor of the Supreme Court of England and Wales; and

(m) words in the singular include the plural, words in the plural include the singular, and words importing the masculine or feminine gender include the neuter.

Explanatory notes

(i)   In connection with the definitions of "controlled trust", see also Rule 9(4) and (5), which provide for other situations where solicitors of the Supreme Court and registered European lawyers are treated as holding money subject to a controlled trust.

(ii)   In connection with the definition of "lawyer", in some jurisdictions there may be uncertainty as to whether a particular profession can be regarded as a "regulated legal profession" in view of the differences in legal and professional structures. In case of doubt solicitors are invited to seek guidance from the Law Society.

Rule 21 – Repeal and commencement

(1)   The Solicitors' Overseas Practice Rules 1987 are hereby repealed.

(2)   These rules shall come into force on 1st September 1990.

Annex G

US Limited Liability Partnerships

(22nd March 2004)

---

1. US LLPs: Accounts and Accountants' Reports for Overseas Practice

Purpose of this note

This note seeks to explain the circumstances in which English solicitors who are partners in a US limited liability partnership (LLP) must comply with the accounting obligations of the Solicitors' Overseas Practice Rules 1990 (SOPR), and must deliver an accountant's report in respect of their US practice.

The nature of US LLPs

Our understanding is that there are three types of US LLP:

- an LLP which has no separate legal personality and is simply a collection of partners carrying on business together (similar to English partnerships) (*category A LLPs*);

- an LLP which has separate legal personality (*category B LLPs*);

- an LLP which has separate legal personality but which can exercise the option to negative the separate legal personality as permitted by law (*category C LLPs*).

So far, we have had to consider the status of New York, Illinois, California, Texas, Minnesota, Georgia and Delaware LLPs against the categories outlined above. The situation would appear to be as follows:

Category A LLPs

LLPs formed under the laws of the states of *New York*, *Illinois* and *Georgia*

Category B LLPs

LLPs formed under the laws of the states of *California*, *Texas* and *Minnesota*

Category C LLPs

LLPs formed under the laws of the state of Delaware

The obligation to deliver an accountant's report

In general terms, section 34 of the Solicitors Act 1974 requires every solicitor who has held or received client money or money subject to a controlled trust to deliver an accountant's report annually. This requirement applies to solicitors whether they practise in England/Wales or overseas. However, a solicitor who does not have to comply with rules 12 or 13 of the SOPR will not have to deliver an accountant's report.

The application of the Solicitors' Overseas Practice Rules 1990

The SOPR apply to a solicitor who practises as such outside England and Wales. Rule 2 of the SOPR deals with the question of whether a solicitor is practising as such from an office outside England and Wales:

- an English solicitor who is a partner in a US LLP, even though he may never physically practise in the US, would be regarded as practising as a solicitor outside England and Wales and would be subject to the SOPR; but

- a solicitor who is dually qualified (for instance as a US attorney) will not be caught by the SOPR if he or she does not do any work reserved to solicitors and is never held out as an English solicitor in respect of the overseas practice of the US LLP.

The obligation to comply with rules 12, 13 and 16 does not arise unless the solicitor or the practice holds money on behalf of clients or subject to a controlled trust. The basic rule is that an English solicitor practising as such must hold accounts, keep records and deliver an accountant's report annually (rules 12, 13, and 16 of SOPR), in relation to all money held or received on behalf of clients, and all money held or received subject to a controlled trust.

However as a result of recent changes to the SOPR there are now two situations in which solicitor partners in a US LLP may be exempt from the accounts requirements:

- If the LLP has separate legal personality and English solicitors do not form a controlling majority of the partners, the solicitor partners are not caught by the accounts requirements – see rule 9(3)(d).

- If the LLP does not have separate legal personality, *and* a controlling majority of the partners are lawyers of other jurisdictions, *and* UK lawyers do not form the largest national group of lawyers in the partnership, the solicitor partners are exempt from the accounts requirements – see rules 12(6) and 13(6).

Note, however, that in either case the accounts requirements will apply to money held or received by an English solicitor as a named trustee.

Implications for solicitors in particular types of US LLP

From the information supplied to us so far, these are the implications for solicitor partners – and hence for the LLP as a whole – in relation to client money or controlled trust money held or received by a US LLP.

- Solicitor partners in *Category A LLPs* (LLPs formed under the laws of the states of New York, Illinois and Georgia):

    - must comply with the accounting provisions of the SOPR and submit an accountant's report if a controlling majority or 50% of the partners are solicitors or if UK lawyers form the largest national group of lawyers in the LLP; but

– are exempt from the accounting provisions of the SOPR, and do not have to submit an accountant's report, if a controlling majority of the partners are non-solicitors and UK lawyers do not form the largest national group of lawyers in the partnership.

- Solicitor partners in *Category B LLPs* (LLPs formed under the laws of the states of California, Texas and Minnesota):

    – must comply with the accounting provisions of the SOPR and submit an accountant's report if solicitors are a controlling majority of the partners; but

    – fall outside the scope of the accounting provisions of the SOPR, and do not have to submit an accountant's report, if solicitors are not a controlling majority of the partners.

- Solicitor partners in *Category C LLPs* (LLPs formed under the law of the state of Delaware) will:

    – fall into Category B if the partners have chosen to retain the LLP's separate legal personality; or

    – fall into Category A if the partners have exercised the election under Delaware law to negative the LLP's separate legal personality.

2. US LLPs: Practice as an MNP in England and Wales

A *Category B LLP* with English solicitor partners cannot practise in England and Wales. To do so would result in the commission of a criminal offence under the Solicitors Act 1974. This applies to an LLP formed under the laws of *California*, *Texas* and *Minnesota*. It also applies to an LLP formed under the law of **Delaware** if the partners have not exercised the election under Delaware law to negative the LLP's separate legal personality.

A *Category A LLP* with English solicitor partners may practise in England and Wales as a multi-national partnership because it has no separate legal personality. This applies to an LLP formed under the laws of *New York*, *Illinois* or *Georgia*. It also applies to an LLP formed under the law of *Delaware* if the partners have exercised the election under Delaware law to negative the LLP's separate legal personality.

Notepaper of a US LLP practising as an MNP in England/Wales

A US LLP which has no separate legal personality, and which is practising in England and Wales as a multi-national partnership, must have on its notepaper a statement that it is regulated by the Law Society. If there are fewer than 20 partners, the LLP's notepaper must carry a list of the partners. If the LLP has more than 20 partners, the notepaper must carry either a list of the partners or a statement that a list of partners is open to inspection at the office. In all cases the list must specify the qualifications of all the partners, so as to distinguish between the solicitor and non-solicitor partners.

22 March 2004

Solicitors and Money Laundering

A Compliance Handbook

Peter Camp

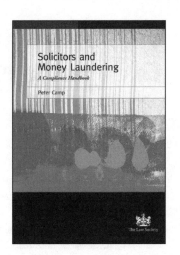

This authoritative handbook clearly demonstrates how the new anti-money laundering laws apply to solicitor's practices. It highlights areas of practice most at risk and gives practical advice on how to introduce anti-money laundering procedures enabling firms to recognize and report suspicious transactions.

The practical nature of the book is enhanced by helpful precedents, guidance material and statutory material, including:

- a precedent money laundering manual
- client identification form, internal reporting form and NCIS reporting forms
- official NCIS guidance on reporting suspicious transactions.

Written by a recognised expert, taking account of the latest Law Society guidelines it is essential reading for solicitors and their professional advisers looking to meet compliance objectives.

Available from Marston Book Services:
Tel. 01235 465 656.

1 85328 920 5
288 pages

The Law Society

Lexcel Practice Excellence Kit

3rd edition

The Law Society

This is the official guide to the Law Society's Lexcel Practice Management Standards. As such it will be essential reading for firms planning to seek or retain Lexcel accreditation and will be valuable to practices looking to improve their office management procedures.

This 3rd edition reflects the new Lexcel Practice Management Standards which came into force in 2004.

The *Lexcel Practice Excellence Kit* contains the:

- *Lexcel Office Procedure Manual* which provides a series of useful templates from which solicitors can prepare a manual for their firm. An accompanying CD-ROM helps you tailor the office manual to meet your firm's requirements.
- *Lexcel Assessment Guide* which sets out the requirements for meeting the revised Lexcel Practice Management Standard and explains the process of Lexcel certification. This edition also includes the assessor's guidelines.

Available from Marston Book Services:
Tel. 01235 465 656.

1 85328 911 6
312 pages
£79.95
April 2004

The Law Society